AF345291

Wild Lakeland

WILD
LAKELAND

BLACK'S
POPULAR
SERIES *of*
COLOUR
BOOKS

GARBURN PASS.

WILD
LAKELAND
PAINTED BY
A. HEATON COOPER
DESCRIBED BY
MACKENZIE MACBRIDE
57265
A&C BLACK LD
4.5.6 SOHO SQUARE, LONDON, W.1.

Published Autumn 1922

CONTENTS

LIST OF ILLUSTRATIONS

By A. HEATON COOPER

WILD LAKELAND

CHAPTER I

LAKELAND UNDER WATER

A highway white with dust that winds amid
  An undulating stretch of breezy down,
Whose ruggedness by spreading ferns is hid—
  Ten miles from any town.

Around the sandy hollows on the heath
  The blackberry vines in prickly clusters run,
And hang, a pendent hedge, where pools beneath
  Lie winking in the sun.

The far-off hills are dotted white with sheep,
  And by the little footpath's rambling course
A tiny beck that murmurs in its sleep
  Trickles beneath the gorse.

'Tis evening now, and in the crystal mere
  Floats the reflected moon—a lotus flow'r—
And from some distant spire ring low and clear
  The bells that chime the hour.

Now like a censer every flower's cup,
　　Swung to and fro exhales a dewy scent,
As all the voices of the night go up
　　In murmurs of content.

And every voice is full of strange appeal,
　　And every wind of mystic whisperings
From lips unseen, as seeking to reveal,
　　The secret soul of things.

For night has made a truce to doubts and fears,
　　And cast her magic spells upon the mind
Which sees a thought in every star and hears
　　It uttered by the wind.

DAVID GOW.

IT is no use denying that the English Lake District has the highest rainfall in our island. It is more watery than any district of the Clyde. With it even Greenock cannot compete. But what then? The rainfall of Lakeland is one of its greatest assets.

To me when the skies are clear and no mists float over the noble hills that stretch across from Helvellyn and Fairfield to the Scawfell group, they have lost their greatest charm. They do not attract so much. Why is this?

Because it is the mist and atmospheric effects which follow each other in never-ending succession, that give to British scenery the mystery and glamour which are the most subtle attractions in art or literature. Their appeal is deepest of all to us humans who are born and live and die in mystery.

When the sky is clear the outlines of the same great hills come nearer to me, as it were; everything is decipherable. The whole secret is proclaimed and, no effort being asked of me, I go home unstimulated in heart and in spirit. My very body does not benefit so much when everything is laid before me and nothing is left for my imagination.

The most subtle of all our sensations, the most lovely of all our poems, the most captivating of all our pictures are those which bring us up against the great shadow—the unknown perhaps the unknowable, who can say!

No traveller returns to tell the secret.

The song, the literature, the art that suggests these things is the greatest art and the greatest literature.

The scenery that gives us this great sense of mystery, of the gigantic, the unseen, the unknown, is nowhere if it is not here when Lakeland is under water. Then the rain fills burn and beck with glittering splendour and there arises a subtle and lovely murmur of the smooth-going Rothay or Derwent, or the thunder of Stock Gill Force when it comes down out of the little stream above after a week's rain, and beats with deep thuds on the rocks below its twin streams, and makes the very air palpitate. The while the wet ground glistens with diamond rain-drops, and a hundred little cascades and rills go hurrying down through the brown beech and birch mast to the crags below.

Attraction again lies in the half tone, the broken colour, the cloudy sky, not in smooth masses.

To move us some subtle beauty of delicate shade is needed—for instance—the smoke blue that fringes the golden yellow on the robin's breast and marks off his delightful tail feathers from the downy part of his back. A canary bird all of one colour is not nearly so charming.

"THE HIGH HILLS ARE A REFUGE FOR THE WILD GOATS" CONISTON.

CHAPTER II

ON THE HIGH HILLS

THEN on the high hills clamber up the wet tracks and visit the lovely loch or " tarn " that lies sheltered in the deep passes and corries, on the sides of the mountains. Only a puff of warm wind is needed and they send up their vapour in billowy clouds that catch every shaft of light, every rosy shade the afternoon sun can lend them—yellow, orange-red, rose-pink and madder-brown. Beneath us, lying low along the fells the mist takes a hundred tones of blue—the smoke blue so baffling to the painter.

Then again, ye grumblers at the rain, consider that a hill in a clear atmosphere has only one outline from each side.

But when it is misty, cloudy ; when there is rain about, Helvellyn, Scawfell, Fairfield have a hundred outlines, ever altering ; ever new ; no two alike all through the long day.

At such a time they claim their kinship with the clouds, and together move and alter into a thousand majestic and mysterious shapes.

> Their step is forth and, ere the day
> Breaks up their leaguer and away,
> Flowers they strew—I catch the scent ;
> Or tone of silver instrument
> Leaves on the wind melodious trace ;
> Yet I could never see their face.[1]

Just to take one example of the wonder and the compelling loveliness that rain imparts to scenery.

Have you ever seen the great hills of the Pennine Chain—Cross Fell, Pen y' Gant, Ingleboro and the others ? They have each a definite form unaltered for this thousand years ; they are bleak, wind-swept, low in colour compared with the richness of the Windermere and Keswick hills. Their soil is very thin and there is sometimes a little growth of short heather which, in the autumn, is black and sombre.

If you choose a wet day and take a walk along the wet, sloping pack-horse road that leads from Orrest Head or from the Troutbeck-Windermere road to the Kirkstone road you will, if you are

---

[1] Emerson.

lucky, get an excellent example upon the nearer of the Pennines of the magical things the rain can do in Lakeland.

The road lies above the Troutbeck Valley to which I refer in another chapter.

At the right-hand turn we are in Garburn Pass, little known though within easy walk of Kendal, Staveley and Windermere, perhaps because the Pennines are bleak and bare and their bareness is too visible under a clear blue sky. In the rain and wind when all nature is astir walk down the short Pass and you will look before you, like Columbus, " with a wild surmise "—for there you will see dimly in the mist, over the great chasm in which lies Kentmere, a giant of the Olympians or the Arabian Nights or of your own far finer, cleaner, Ossianic legends ; a giant vague of outline, shrouded by mist and whole battalions of clouds ; his front partly visible here and there, tipped with pale yellow light. Deep valleys lie at his feet and sides, shutting him off from weak humanity typified in the fragments of Kentmere village far below in its dark Pass, once occupied by a lake. The giant we see is of the Whernside, Pen y' Gant and Ingleboro group.

It is a great and rememberable sight and the feast of colour—the short red bracken, faded heather, yellow mosses and faded chamois velvet grass, as you turn back to look at Garburn Pass itself, will also remain with you.

I was told afterwards that we should have made Staveley our starting-point, but I ask no more than what I saw from Garburn Pass.

CHAPTER III

THERE are not many places from which you can see five or six mountain ranges by simply turning your head from east to west. Yet that is what I can do as I write, and I have chosen the spot above the Gale at Ambleside, only three minutes' walk from where I live, because from it I can see five or six different cloud effects over as many mountain ranges, and it is the cloud effects we in this prosaic country neglect. Yet they are our peculiar possession.

To the west is the hill called the Sergeantman which overlooks Grasmere's flowery valley and joins hands with Langdale's Pikes. Round his long shoulder dark bluish-black clouds are moving; and, seen over the green top of Loughrigg below, are a black hill and a distant line of grey mountain. Just above them there hangs a little streak of light grey cloud its whiteness making the mountain-tops clear at that part and giving them a fine touch of mystery. To the south, over Waterhead and Brathay, brilliant white clouds hover, lit by the sinking sun into unpaintable brightness.

To the north is the grand range which includes Nab Scar, Lord Crag, Heron Pike, Great Rigg and Fairfield. It is this range whose noble outlines make Ambleside so unique and lovely. Over these first four two perpendicular lines of dark clouds are slowly hovering, while a brilliant touch of light rests upon the westernmost shoulder of Nab Scar.

Over Fairfield the lines of cloud are densely blue, long and ridged, giving the great hill distance and solemnity. Under it and Great Rigg, in the valley, is a blue shadow soft as haze, while over Fairfield's right shoulder an irregular patch of green sky is broken suddenly by the beautiful outlines, now clearly visible in detail, of High and Low Pike, which lie to the west and slope nobly, in a running line, towards the Rydal Valley. On their Scandale side the two peaks form a curve which resembles in form the great precipice of Striding Edge.

All these mountain ranges are dim to-night ; touched with mystery ; changing momently. In front of me, a little to the east, is the great broad base of Snarker Moss with Snarker Pike above. The top of the hill, in full sunlight, forms a great green and cultivated contrast to the wild rough mountain character of all the rest of the landscape from west to east.

Above it is another skyscape—a big patch of blue, and resting yet moving imperceptibly over the Pike, the drifting, shifting, billowy clouds. At the foot of the great hill is the valley of the river Stock the murmur of which is very delightful.

One other hill range lies to the right of where the Kirkstone Pass is marked by trees, pale yellow-green larch and dark firs. Over Stock Gill's grand Force or waterfall, and further east, is a blue sky with a few sentinel clouds here, grey and white, there touched by the lessening sunlight.

On the extreme right (east) rising in a rugged flowing line to his topmost crag, and somewhat barren in appearance, is Wansfell. In five minutes the whole cloudscape has moved, but in the western part lying over beyond the Sergeantman, where in the heart of the great hills, the peaks of

Scawfell attract and draw the clouds, we still see
the grandest forms, full of the fine reflected lights
—silver and blue and grey.

And now a cloud of uncommon shape has driven
in on the extreme west; it has square outlines
like the form of a great castle or black pile of
masonry. It glides into the shape of three
close huge peaks; and to the north in the distance, over Kirkstone way, we can now see the
form of Caudle Moor which alone has caught on
its sides the rose-yellow hues of the setting sun.

CHAPTER IV

THERE are one or two beauties of the Lakeland hills which are apt to be overlooked because they are merely seen casually and are not realised and considered. We may admire a thing but it carries us mentally a step further if we know why we instinctively admire it.

Amongst the beauties of Lakeland I put second to none the forms, the outlines of its hills.

Many mountain ranges are so worn down by time and tempest that all their forms are blunt and flattened. They have no peaks, no splintered crags, no beautiful cone - like tops. The downs of the south of England, the Pennine mountains including the spur that runs from them westward into Yorkshire and Lancashire, are notable rather for their mass and bulk than for their graceful

or splendid outlines. Ingleboro, and Crossfell
seen from Ouseby on the western plain below,
are notable exceptions. Speaking generally these
heights are far behind the Lakeland mountains in this respect, though they possess the
beauty that belongs to great masses.

What could be finer, for instance, than the
noble outlines of the hills that form the three
glens at the head of Windermere ? This group
is especially fine ; it includes Rydal Fell, the
shoulder of Nab Scar, Lord Crag and Heron
Pike also the splendid round cone of Great Rigg,
highest of the group, which reaches 2513 feet.
Advancing well into the foreground, on the
opposite side of the valley, come the opposing
ridge of Scandale Fell and the sharp wedge of
High Pike, with the graceful curve of precipitous
cliff to which I have referred, in its rear, and the
sharp point of Low Pike in front.

Then how welcome a relief is the long sloping
horizontal of the giant Fairfield running across
the same valley from Great Rigg to Hart Crag.
The latter's fine cone, by the way, is not seen from
many points, but it is really a part of Fairfield.
The best view of it I know is from near Fox How
going towards Pelter Bridge.

SPRINKLING TARN AND GREAT GABLE.

The country at the foot of this great assembly of bare, often snow-covered peaks is rich with splendid woodlands and fat green fields and gardens.

The Splintered Peaks of Scawfell

What a contrast is the frugal setting of the great central range of Lakeland to Ambleside's rich meadows, its kingcups, buttercups, coverlets of hyacinth bells, wall-tops overlapped with yellow stonecrop! How different is it from Rydal's broom-sheltered burns; copper and red beeches seen against pale-green larches; gold-green oaks, and blue-green ash trees; from Grasmere's wealth of cultivated flowers, its valleys below the great fells, filled brim full with woodlands!

Very different from the rounded hill-tops about the Ambleside region also are the outlines of the shattered peaks of this great central group set in their treeless, bird-shunned wilderness of crags and precipices. Yet the forms we find there are of marvellous beauty. I will just remind the reader of a few of them. To their value from the climbing point of view I am quite indifferent. Of the wonderful beauty of their forms; their majesty and grace, their unutterable silence and peace I am an ardent worshipper.

Scawfell Pinnacle

One of the noblest of them is Scawfell Pinnacle, with the deep shadows of Steep Gill chasm and those of its lower peaks casting its jagged lances into grand relief. How superbly it throws its head back, its whole surface full of lovely shadows and half tones both upright and across, bringing out the ragged, terrible crags below.

Bowfell and its Buttress

I have looked on Bowfell daily for a whole year and have seen him from many sides with his noble partners, and I can confirm the statement some one has made that he is grand from any point of view. But to me finest is the distant view where the vast bulk of the mass to which he belongs is contrasted against those mystical battlements of his great neighbour Crinkle Crags, with their suggestion that the high gods dwell behind them. For a nearer view, for wonderful grace, strength and the repose and restfulness

THE SCAWFELLS FROM HARDKNOTT PASS.

that belong to strength, next in loveliness is the sight of Bowfell Buttress from below.

The Pillar Rock

The Pillar Rock is another of the climber's favourites, and the view of it a little way off is very grand, especially the castle-like pinnacles on its eastern side and the beautiful, vertical lines of the cliffs on the west or High Man side.

On the summit there is a piece of slate on which climbers used to write their names and there was for a long time a tin box also, in which they later put their cards.

The Low Man from which the High Man springs is a grand cliff and the north side and the crags seen from the north-east are stately, varied, and full of interesting detail.

The Scawfell Group

Very imposing is the view of the Scawfell group from Wastdale Head and Great Gable; their precipitous sides, their vast bulk, their deep black gullies and their grand cliffs.

Only the red mosses and the red colour of the

Screes—those splendid crags—relieve the severity of the scene.

From Scawfell Pike, the highest peak of all, we can see the Scottish Border hills, Skiddaw and Crosthwaite; the Helvellyn range including Fairfield; Ill Bell and Wansfell, the Langdale Pikes, Bowfell; while to the east and south lies Ingleboro. To the west we have Coniston Old Man, Hardknot, Eskdale, the Furness hills and the sea at Morecambe. Also Lancaster Castle and sometimes Snowdon.

The hills of the central range are very well seen—Great Gable, Kirkfell, the Steeple Rock, Red Pike, High Stile, the Pillar and beyond Crummock Water, Buttermere, with Grasmere, and Causey Pikes. Below us is Sty Head Tarn. Altogether it is a wonderful scene and the utter barrenness of the rocks, save for the red mosses, is in striking contrast to the green valleys of the Esk, Miter, Dunnerdale and Borrowdale, lying below us.

CHAPTER V

WINTER IN LAKELAND

Weird the sound the owlets make,
Blackened branches creak and break,
Yet the new grass we have crossed
Shows up greenly through the frost,
And the brackens, ten feet high,
Make a glorious canopy
For the trees on which they die.
Strange when Winter's hands lie spread
Lifeless 'neath the coverlid,
That Nature brings us such a dower !
Here's the holly tree in flower !
Never was there lovelier sight,
Tipped each leaf with constant light ;
And red berries half concealed
Like some secret stand revealed,
As the writing on the wall
Of Belshazzar's fated hall ;
But with them there comes no dread—
Fair hopes written there instead !
Token that though Nature frowns,
She plants wild-flowers on the downs,
Bids the snow-drop sweet to rise,
Sends clear stars to winter skies,

Brightest colour to the ferns ;
Purest showers to Winter's burns ;
Sunniest brown to Autumn sheaves,
Reddest hues to falling leaves ;
Whitest mantle to the snow,
Cleanest winds that ever blow
Such as summers never know.

   .   .   .   .   .   .

Lo she lends us solemn hint
In giving death the noble tint
Of the blood that fills her veins,
The crimson rose her heart contains.

MacKenzie MacBride.

THE coloured things among the dark branches of the woods—the berries of the holly, the hawthorn and the guelder rose, are not all that is left to us in a Lakeland winter. The grey mists often hang heavily, the rain is plentiful and all nature seems sodden and depressed yet a couple of hundred feet above our gossiping little town things take on another aspect.

A village without folk in its streets is at times a little depressing, but 200 feet up above the town and the mist, there is plenty of life. The birds are very busy, the starling and the robin are friendly and the finches though less bold, are grateful for human society everywhere. The starling carries on his music-hall kind of ventriloquial entertainment every morning and all the

day. The daws too are amusing and pour a
constant shower of sticks a foot in length down
my bedroom chimney. The robin comes to
one's very feet for crumbs looking as dapper as
a sergeant-major of the Seaforths, or the Argyll
and Sutherlands.

And there, away from the towns and the mist
we find winter in its coloured clothing more
gorgeous than the Queen of Sheba herself. A
cloak of the rose-pink bracken to which I have
referred, covers great part of the hills, and
chamois-yellow grass, smooth as velvet, brightened
and relieved by emerald-green patches, covers the
other half, while, far up, on towards the bare
crags, are black patches of faded heather giving
strength and shade and contrast to the whole.

Around there is a great silence made more
impressive by the roar of Stock Gill Force that
leaps from the level side of the hill, over the
precipice to the great lake below. If we follow
the stream we find it has also a wealth of colour
and of light and shade : here it is pale yellow,
there deep amber like a cairngorm stone ; now
pale emerald, and, where the sun catches it,
glittering with brightness like a silver casket.
Its sounds are as varied ; yonder it runs seething

over pebbles and great stones ; there in the deep pools, it has a rich contralto note.

Along the magnificent Windermere, Ambleside, Grasmere road we can always get a very feast of colour—the bracken on a hundred hills ; the brown-red leaves on those splendid beech hedges that fringe the road ; the rust-red wrack of the longer bracken and saplings in the woods. All these things, and the wealth of foliage on the hills, on the cliffs of the Rothay and Brathay valleys and on the Furness Fells opposite are far more full of colour in September, November, December and February when " the sedge has withered by the lake and the harvest's done," than in May, June and July because the sedge and all or most other green things are in death nobler of hue than in their prime.

CHAPTER VI

THE Kirkstone is easily the most famous pass amongst the English mountains and always attracts strangers. This is not because of its beauty, when compared with other roads in the same neighbourhood. Its scenery cannot be named with that of the Grasmere or Skelwith Bridge and Coniston roads or the splendid road over Red Bank, or the Windermere Road. The Kirkstone Pass suggests rather the bleak Pennines or the Yorkshire moors.

Nor is the side of the valley through which the road runs the better side. The views of the distant hills to the west seen from the Stockgill-Grove Farm road on the opposite, eastern, side are amongst the finest in the district. The Kirkstone is really to be regarded more as a curiosity, and as the Pass which has seen of all passes, the most battles—between Scots and English. The most difficult part to climb is that up North road Ambleside, to Seathwaite and Round Hill Farm, soon after leaving Ambleside and the village of Edinburgh. From here we can see the valley of the Stock and the old farm-houses of Low and Middle Grove on the other side of the bare, bleak slopes of Wansfell.

Higher up we get a raised valley of great width over which is a fine view of Ill Bell. There is not much colour in the scene—bleakness and barrenness everywhere around.

At Sunny Side cottages there is a gate to the old pack-horse road which leads to Round Hill Farm and across the bottom of the valley to Middle Grove. There is not much else of interest till one reaches " The Traveller's Rest " inn at the dreary summit where the Windermere-Troutbeck road joins the Kirkstone road. Here we get a view of Red Screes with a grand corrie in its side where soft blue shadows continually abide contrasting with the rich red rock of the mountain itself. Rounding the point we soon see the difficult path which leads by Caiston Glen, at the head of Scandale, past the other side of Red Screes to the Kirkstone road. The view of the

angular lines of the Screes as you reach Caiston top from Scandale is very imposing. Brothers Water is also seen far below.

On the right we have a good view of John Bell's Banner—the triangle-shaped side of the great hill on the right which is striped with wonderful orange-red blaeberry and pink-red bracken suggesting a banner. On the left-hand side we soon come to the old Smiddy, now in ruins, which was used when the mines were worked at this spot. The Smiddy stands on the old pack-horse track on the other side of the stream close to the new road on which we are walking.

Now we get a view of Brothers Water and, turning our faces to the road we have come down, we have a good view of the three great cone-topped hills that so finely fill the valley at this point. The right-hand one is Hartsop Dodd, the next Middle Dodd, and the third High Hartsop Dodd. The repetition of the ugly name Dodd does not suggest an imaginative peasantry but the scene is very fine. There is an Eastern look about these grand peaks, a suggestion of Sinbad in the valley of diamonds. We are, in fact, getting out of the stony, bleak, rather depressing wilderness into one of those rich and lovely and sheltered scenes which the Lady of the Lakes keeps up her sleeve to astonish us with when we become scornful. We exclaim " Behold how poverty-stricken ! " and a moment later she pours the wealth of Golconda into our laps.

The day is very hot and the green Hartsop valley with its woods and water, is welcome and refreshing. My companion whose very appearance—six foot two and " lean and lank and brown as is the ribbed sea-sand "—suggests Sinbad, now actually produces diamonds of another kind in the shape of a tea-kettle, a spirit-lamp—teetotal spirits—a milk-bottle, some pies, sandwiches and also a custard. He leads the way to a spot shaded from the wind down under the bank of the Caudle burn or beck—a delightful stream. He lights the spirit-lamp and goes off to get some cream from Caudle Beck Farm.

We sat down in the shade out of the burning Sinbad's country kind of sun, and ate the pies, the sandwiches and the custard cake which last was, I fear, my friend's undoing for he had a sick headache for the rest of the day.

After visiting a friend's cottage and arranging for tea, we went down to Hartsop Hall and thence to the foot of Brothers Water and, taking a rowing boat—the only one—we pushed out and spent three hours on that lovely lake. My friend, Sinbad, an enthusiastic fisherman, commenced to lash the water with his line and in three hours succeeded in catching three fat trout. During these hours he seemed worried and anxious—a thing unusual with him—but whether this anxiety was due to the scarcity of fish or to the custard I could not make out.

CHAPTER VII

SINBAD IN THE VALLEY OF DIAMONDS

HERE at Hartsop and Kirkstone Foot we have come right to the back of the Ambleside and Rydal region and have a new and commanding object in full view—Dove Crag. Indeed it dominates the whole glen in which we find ourselves, huge, black, full of deep shadows, threatening, this grim giant with his terrible cliffs and sharp-pointed neighbour crags.

Later as we get down into the valley we have also a good view of Brothers Water looking very blue in the distance a little way further down the valley.

From the Lake we see to great advantage the pointed cone of John Bell's Banner, otherwise known as High Hartsop Dodd, and turn from this hill to the two other volcano-like peaks, and then continuing the semicircle, grandest of all come to Dove Crag and his neighbours. The whole valley head is, in fact, filled by those awe-inspiring and fantastic shapes.

And now the glittering sun has put out the blue and taken possession of the lake and we row up towards the head where the Hartsop beck flows into it between two pretty promontories of grey stones.

Along the head of the lake the bleached sticks of last year's sedge make a fine contrast to the clear brown water and the low green alder and thorn bushes of which there are great masses here.

Looking up the lake there is a shadow now on Middle Dodd peak while the cones of his two companions are in brilliant sunshine. Down the lake we have a good view of Place Fell on Ullswater ; and of High Street, on the top of which steep and difficult hill, there is the ancient Roman road—undoubtedly Roman this one. All the mountains on that side are very bare of trees but on the other side, we have the wooded packhorse road and a wealth of greenery.

Despite the absence of wood there is no lack of colour on the hills at the head of the Pass. At their top and down their sides they have, like John Bell's Banner, patches of browns and bright yellows like velvet from the blaeberry plants and mosses, which give a striking and uncommon beauty.

Here and there the new sedge grass, very pale green, is showing through the faded brown reeds of last year on the margin of the lake ; a fine bit of colour.

The Lake itself has ever-changing hues ; here it is green and its wavelets are edged with deep blue shadows. The sky is very blue with very white masses of cloud here and there. A sand-piper has just flashed past us across the stream. Sinbad, my friend, is industriously and rather sadly fishing.

The hills towards Ullswater up the lake look well from here. They are deeply lined with cliffs, and patches of pale greens among grasses a little darker and remains of pink bracken, give them a touch of warmth.

These hills, by the way, are very much like the excellent drawings in black and white made by the Ambleside artist William Green, fifty years ago. British art may have progressed, in some, nay in many, ways, but it has lost the power of closely rendering landscape in black and white shown by Green.

The yellow-brown reeds now again make a fine contrast with the blue water. A mist is creeping solemnly up over Dove's grim crags and deep shadows. A sea-gull is flying across the lake. I notice the dried black heather of last year on the hill above Hartsop Hall.

On the opposite side from the water, we have a good view of the little village of Hartsop right below the rocky wilderness of High Street, so strangely chosen by the Romans for their camp or rallying ground all those centuries ago and yet so unaltered to-day.

For, no doubt the yellow reeds flanked the blue lake in those days ; gorgeous blaeberry mixed with yellow mosses spread themselves on John Bell's Banner ; the sandpiper flitted past with his pretty piping note ; the sea-gulls flew down the glen towards Ullswater, and the fishes often refused to bite ; and though my excellent Sinbad was not there—unless in a previous incarnation, the Roman sentinels sometimes did their fishing without catching any fish and felt sad therefore, or from having dined, if not on custard, at least not wisely but too well.

CHAPTER VIII

WHAT are the limits of the privileges we are to allow to the sportsman ?

If we would preserve Nature with the wild creatures of the woods and lakes and the birds of the air, this is a question which will have to be very carefully weighed.

I am myself unable to enjoy an " amusement " that brings terror and death to Nature's beautiful creatures which, though they prey upon each other, just as men do, generally speaking bring swift, and therefore, merciful end to their victims, while men bring often a slow lingering death to the fox, the otter, the hare.

Only the other day I was told by a friend in Ambleside of an otter—that gallant, witty and pretty little fellow—who was hunted by a pack of twenty hounds and as many sportsmen. After a long chase they cornered him in an awkward

SHAP ABBEY AND FELLS

pool which was cut off from the deep stream above by a " jamb " or side pillar of rock.

Well he dived so often and so quickly that both hounds and men were tired. Then some one pointed out that if they kept the little swimmer under water long enough, he would be forced to come up at last for air and then the twenty hounds plus the twenty gallant gentlemen could kill him. They waited.

At last the otter rose, gasping for air and scrambled on to a small ledge of rock where he quickly lost all that delightful vivacity, his splendid swimming powers, his quick wit and sparkling eye—that merry little fellow was killed and mangled—by the Huns.

Owing to this kind of " sport " the otter has become rather rare in Lakeland, though I think I know where I could see one, swimming out in deep water, with a wave such as a steamer makes in front of him, and his tail, moving in a semi-circle, acting the part of a steam-propeller, much as a fox uses his brush to increase his speed when desperately hard pressed.

The otter will alas ! soon disappear from the Lake District but he is not the only one of the interesting animals that have been thus persecuted.

A good many years ago Richard Jefferies gave a list of the birds and other creatures which we have almost killed off.

Many of these (probably all) were certainly useful—the owl for instance. Though I am glad to say the neglect of sport during the War allowed the owls to recruit their numbers, and during that time I knew of one which took up its quarters in a large garden in the very heart of London, which was much enclosed by walls and surrounded by other open spaces.

So far as I have seen the magpie has quite disappeared from the Lake District. A most amusing fellow he is with a kind of cockney wit about him, and he is ever ready to " pal on " with mankind.

The raven was plentiful in the Lake District. To-day he is only seen in the recesses of the mountains.

Jefferies gave a list of creatures that had been persecuted out of existence in the interests of the pheasant shooter—the pine marten, polecat, eagle, buzzard, falcon, kite, horned owl, harrier and raven.

The buzzard may now be seen again in the Lake District as pointed out in another chapter.

The badger or brock, whose name in its Keltic form exists in so many place names in England and Scotland—Brockwell, Brockbank, Brocklehurst, Ibrox (Glasgow) has in wild Lakeland become quite extinct save in one landowner's preserve. These names show how common it once was.

CHAPTER IX

THE SACRIFICE TO TROUT

But perhaps most destruction has been done in the interests of that voracious and cannibalistic fish the trout, who devours not only the spawn of his neighbours and of his own cousins and aunts but also their infant children!

Here is a list of the beautiful and interesting creatures that have been persecuted in the interests of the trout. The list was given by Jefferies many years ago. They total sixteen in all—the otter—of special interest; pike, perch; heron, that beautiful bird! the kingfisher regarded as the handsomest bird bred in the island; the owl, one of the most serviceable to the farmers; the pretty moorhen; the coot, grebe, diver, and the wild-duck—how charming to see a party of them on the wing!—one in advance and two following. The teal, the dipper, the land rat, the water rat.

This makes fifteen. The sixteenth and last, is the swan, so precious to Lakeland, so lovely and so dignified that it deserves a chapter to itself in which we may consider its claims. For the swan is a national pet and, like the dog, has citizen's rights if not a vote. We must remember too the rights of the people who sail up Windermere and see the sixteen splendid birds of which Bowness boasts, curveting round the prow of their steamer waiting for the visitors to feed them.

Now if the belief that condemned all these creatures to destruction in the interests of a single species of fish were well founded and it became a question as to whether the one fish was to disappear or the sixteen other creatures sent by Nature doubtless not merely out of idleness, I should say it were better to lose the one than the sixteen which included things so interesting as an otter and so beautiful as a swan.

But when one comes to make inquiries on this point from those who should know what do they say? Mr. John Watson of Kendal, a lifelong fisherman in Lakeland, says of our little friend, " A great deal of un-natural history has been written about the otter . . . careful observation goes to show that eels and fresh-water crayfish constitute a large portion of its food . . . I have invariably found trout most abundant near the haunts of the otter. The otter destroys fewer fish than is generally supposed. This may appear a bold statement, but it is a fact. It is confirmed by water bailiffs, otter hunters and fish poachers. Of forty-five otters killed in hunting, in two only were there the remains of fish food and this consisted of eels —deadly enemies to trout streams or salmon rivers . . . I have in my mind's eye a famous river reach where otters and plenty of trout exist side by side." He adds, "Where the fastnesses of the former are impregnable, disease is foreign to the stream. The economy of the otter ought not to be overlooked in connection with sport and our fish supply. Probably its increasing rarity has much to do with salmon disease, as had the extermination of the larger birds of prey with grouse disease. A falcon always takes the easiest chance and so does an otter. In each case they kill out the weakest and thereby tend to stamp out disease. . . . I am convinced that on a trout-stream otters do much more good than harm."

Again the dipper has been made rare on false pretences like the otter if Frank Buckland was to be believed: he said that you might as well shoot a swallow skimming over a turnip-field as a dipper over the spawning grounds. This view Mr. John Watson considers to be the right one. What the dipper actually does take for breakfast are the eggs of the dragon-fly, May-fly and stone-fly, which flies are, Mr. Watson says, " among the chief enemies of trout spawn."

Richard Jefferies' list is not complete for to it might be added the dotterel which has been hunted down, not on account of any iniquity, but because its feathers are mistakenly believed by anglers to be of special value in the making of flies.

CHAPTER X

Doon the burn Davie love,
Doon the burn Davie love,
Gang doon the burn Davie love
And I will follow thee !

W. CRAWFORD.

ONE of the old-world spots in Lakeland is reached
by taking the road on the left from the foot of
Smithy Brow, Ambleside, and on through the
splendidly wooded " Nook," past the kennels of
the Coniston Hunt on the hill to the right,
till you reach Lower Scandale or Nook End
bridge at Nook End. Over the bridge passed
the old pack-horse track, and still goes, despite
obstructions, across the face of Scandale Hill
to Rydal Fell which it crosses, and on through
the stable yard of Rydal Hall to Grasmere. But
there is another ancient right of way after crossing
Nook bridge. This track follows the Scandale

ANGLE TARN, ESK HAUSE.

burn right up the Glen, through a bit of fairy-
land. As Prior (1862) says :—" Undine herself
might have emerged from the grotto-pool of this
solitude." Presently the river sweeps round finely
and there is a succession of six or seven waterfalls
small but very lovely. Keeping low down by the
burn—a very wet walk it is, by the way, but well
worth doing—you can cross the iron bridge at the
intake of the Manchester Corporation, and get a
good view of the brown stream gurgling and
hurrying along under the green leaves. The
old right of way crossed the river hereabouts by
a public bridge and led you on to the Scandale
Glen and Patterdale road. As the whole of that
road is of great beauty and interest, it is best to
leave it for a separate walk.

So close down by the burn in that leafy
paradise, we pick our way. By this time we are
under high cliffs and banks clad with larch and
fir, and the swish of them, mingled with the
murmur of the stream, makes you think of
far-off Perthshire or Argyll.

Keeping along the west bank we cross some
very wet bracken and come under the small
hut of the stone quarries on the other side. The
woods are still very rich and lovely and we get

peeps of distant hills. Scandale Fell and Low Pike, his partner, are now above us.

And so, after a long but delightful walk in an intimate contact with the woodlands such as we cannot get anywhere else in the neighbourhood in this perfection, we make our way into the open, just above the small but steep and rocky waterfall at ancient Sweden Bridge. On a week day you probably will not meet a soul till you get to the bridge itself. There you may find a lover and his lass, but you will not be crowded out or blinded with motor dust.

The water of the Scandale burn is drunk by the town of Ambleside and none better can be found. Some of it is also taken all the way to Manchester because a pipe of the Thirlmere scheme of that city crosses the Scandale Glen lower down as has been said.

Upper Scandale and Caiston

Just beyond the nice old bridge a ruin may be seen. It is, or has been, what is called a hoghouse. A hog is a sheep of two years, and the name Hogarth or Hoggart (Hogherd) means a shepherd.

At the bridge on the rising ground the old

footroad runs across several stiles to the field above Nook End bridge over which you can get back into Ambleside.

Caiston Glen and Red Screes

From the continuation of the footpath just above the waterfall we get a fine view down towards Windermere and the hills to the south. This is the view that John Martin the painter of " The Last Judgment," " Sadak in search of the Waters of Oblivion " and other pictures in their day strange and new, according to local tradition took for his " Plains of Heaven." Certainly it is a wide-spreading and commanding view.

The road now leaves the burn and runs along under Snarker Pike, the hill that looks so fine from the Hawkshead road. On the left we have Scandale Fell with its summit High Pike. The road, which is very wet and has become a mere track, takes another bend to the east as we approach the great hill called Red Screes.

The scenery at this part of the glen is bare and bleak with little colour. We are now approaching a wall of hills the shapes of which do not declare themselves from this height, but seen from Kirkstone Foot, nearly 1800 feet below, they are among the grandest in the Lake district. They number three, the nearest one is Little Hart Crag (2091) which we have on our left as we come to the edge of the wall ; the second and grandest of all is Dove Crag (2500), and the furthest one is Hart Crag the great eastern shoulder of Fairfield to which reference has already been made, which reaches 2690 feet. Of these we can see little, but they form part of the great wall which fills the end of Scandale Glen.

Keeping along past the old sheepfold on the left, we strike across towards a small gap in the great wall I have described, just below the Screes. There is no view, all is shut in until we enter the gap and then one of those great sights I have referred to, which even in recollection appeal to one's imagination, is spread before us.

The Gap in the opening to Caiston Glen is hardly a glen ; really it is a narrow gully or precipitous channel lying between Little Hart Crag and Red Screes. But what a prospect it opens to us—the Kirkstone road with Brothers Water ; Hartsop and its meadows and woodlands ; and, filling up the right side of Caiston Gully is the heavy-shouldered giant, Red Screes, with its series of terrific chasms, their wonderful red colour making a most subtle and alluring contrast to the bleached and withered grass of the Glen itself. It is a great sight and one which has the element of surprise about it to an unusual degree.

CHAPTER XI

FROM Caiston Glen there is an extensive view towards Brock Crags, Angle Tarn, difficult of approach, the Pikes, Boardale Hause, Place Fell (2154) Bannerdale, and Martindale Forest. The view to the east is, however, shut in by Red Screes and Middle Dodd the cone-topped northern end of the mass of which Red Screes forms the southern part. On the left stands High Hartsop Dodd which forms the cone-topped northern end of the mass of which Little Hart Crag is part.

The descent of nearly 2000 feet into Kirkstone Foot down Caiston Glen is very wet and rough and the ground is full of small rills which, hidden in the grass, may easily cause a sprained ankle.

Even if the descent is made it is difficult to find the way on to the Kirkstone road owing to

the many walls you have to climb and the frail
bridge you may not easily find. And, well the
country is not very pleasant or homely just here.
We have not yet got out of the bare wilderness of
Scandale Head and Kirkstone Foot, into rich and
romantic Hartsop, nor can we see the Arabian-
Night like hills down which we have plunged.
They have not yet got distance in which to group
themselves. Then the walk back to Ambleside
by the main road is a rather dreary and very
tough one.

So that on the whole it is better far not to
descend Caiston Glen, unless you are making for
Patterdale, but to go back the way you came
through Scandale, only instead of keeping by
the burn, take the road on the other, south-east,
side of the glen and you will have an easy downhill road all the way to Ambleside. On this road
are some of the finest views of the great western
hills.

When you return to high Sweden Bridge you
take the road to the left, and, after passing through
the first gate, you begin to get some grand
views of High Pike. From the quarry hut the
view of the blue hills above the trees which fill
the deep and narrow channel of the Scandale

burn, is very fine. And later over the shoulder of High Pike as you look north you get more distant hills bathed sometimes in yellow light. A little further on, at the second gate, you have a fine larch wood.

High Pike's blue haze acquires a splendid setting when the young larch comes out in its warm yellow hue, or when it is passing into the soft purple brown of autumn. At the swing gate with the larch wood on your left, all the time looking back, the scene and the sound of the murmuring waters down below, are like a chapter out of the West Highlands.

Then, beyond the last gate, the road rising all the time, turns round south and from the height you, looking back, get a delightful glimpse of the road itself, down which we have just walked, with the great hills on the left all the way.

But even these views of High Pike are not the best things Scandale has to justify our choosing two walks in it to one in Kirkstone Pass. For now there breaks upon us a magnificent view of the Langdales in all their splendour, and beyond them great Bowfell. Running along this east side of them is a dark glen which throws up with mysterious grandeur the long line of

STAKE PASS AND BOWFELL.

jagged hills that end in the wonderful and delightful battlements, which we call by the silly name of Crinkle Crags and Shelter Crags. The less prosaic Welsh or Scots or Irish would have called them Caisteel Abhail (Castcheel Avail) that is the Peaks of the Castles or by a high-sounding word like Schiehallion or Blencathara.

The view is made more magnificent by the fact that from the road we are travelling, which is some 800 feet above sea-level, all the land slopes downward towards the linked valleys of the Rothay, the Brathay and the Langdale Beck. This fact gives the appearance of monstrous height to the group of hills we have in front of us at this point. Into these dim, mysterious valleys great crags run down like buttresses, bold and massive, their lines suggestive of strength and power, and at one spot in the very centre of the gap between these hill slopes, which come from either side of the great glens, we see the whole form of Bowfell.

Then we must not forget that between us and this Gargantuan land we have sloping down from our very feet, the greenest of grass lands, where the lambs skip and the cattle graze in summer time ; for we are on the very edge of Ambleside

7

and Rydal's rich valley, filled with splendid woods and cornlands and flowers. From them we can, in contrast, here lift our eyes to yon savage and mystic wilderness.

Ellerig and Chapel Hill

And now we come to the first house on the road, long since turned into a hay barn. It stands in a grand position on the highest part of the road.

On the other side of the watershed we now have views towards Windermere and across the fields towards Kirkstone. After passing the remains of two or three other dwelling-houses now turned into hog-houses, we again get a glimpse of the charming neighbourhood of Nook End with its magnificent trees and reach the first house. This belongs to Mr. Thomas Bell of Ambleside. From the gate on the right-hand side there is a fine view through the trees, of the round cone of Great Rigg towards the west.

We now descend into Ellerig, a very pretty, leafy bit of Ambleside, and soon get some very good views of the town, the church, of Loughrigg and of the Brathay valley.

In a few moments we are at Chapel Hill on the top of which, close to the church, sits like a hen guarding her chickens, the old manor-house it is generally called, or a very well-to-do statesman's house it may have been. What is more to the point it is quite the most interesting house between Ambleside and Troutbeck, and the very best specimen of the home of the well-to-do of the late sixteenth or early seventeenth century, in this part of Westmorland, so far as my observation has gone. It is bigger than the house of the Walmsley family, and has been divided into five tenements. It has not been altered out of its original character, fortunately, and I hope may never be. Next to it is a huge barn which was, much later, the village school, in which Hartley Coleridge was one of the masters. The site of the old manor-house as of Chapel Hill generally is very fine. It formed the chief part of the ancient town of Ambleside. The old manor-house was recently sold but it found a keenly appreciative buyer fortunately, in an artist, Miss Grundy.

CHAPTER XII

New Value of Old Roads and Footpaths

Up to the coming of the railway and the canal
all the traffic was carried on pack-horses, a fact
we are a little apt to forget. Trains of these
animals laden with goods, went once or twice
weekly and sometimes oftener between the
villages and towns. The trains of pack-horses
leaving Kendal, for instance, by the old road over
Hardknot Pass for Whitehaven, numbered as
many as 300. The leading horse wore above his
head in a kind of collar, a bell which signalled the
approach of the procession to the buyers in the
country houses and farms as the traders advanced
over the fells, much as in the towns, an interesting
survival, the muffin man's bell, does to - day.
The ancient pack-horse roads still remain on the
hills ; portions of them were often included in

the new roads by MacAdam, Telford and other engineers.

Of these roads there is a good specimen in use for instance, leading from Troutbeck to Ambleside by High Skelgill. This road still continues till it joins the old Ambleside main road at Low Fold, Fisherbeck and Low Field and Gale Firs, where it descends at Gale Lodge into the old village and turns up North road to Scandale and Ellerig. Its ancient main track as shown in old maps—the Ordnance of 1865 for instance, continued over Low Scandale Bridge at Nook End, Ambleside, and went through where the present stone wall now obstructs it, completely .barring the way. The road swept round Rydal valley on the high ground and passed through the stable-yard of Rydal Hall to Rydal Mount. It then continued and still does so, at the top side of Rydal Mount to Grasmere via White Moss and Dove cottage. At Rydal Mount road it is crossed by the ancient right of way up the Rydal burn and by the right of way over Nab Scar.

The old villages of Ambleside and Smithy Brow, North Road and Chapel Hill stand upon the southern part of this road and the whole of the traffic of this side of the valley, as Miss Armit pointed out, went along it. The present main Rydal road did not then exist.

At Rydal this ancient road was joined by the old pack-horse track which can be seen in parts beside the newer road, and is in some places included in the newer road, from Pelter Bridge by Fox How to Clappersgate, Rothay Bridge, Waterhead and the Roman Camp at Borrans, Ambleside.

Before the building of the present lodge of Rydal Park in the Rydal road there was another ancient right of way called the Church Path from the main road near Lesketh How, across Rydal Park ; this track also, came out in the stable - yard of Rydal Hall. For the benefit of the owners of Rydal this was moved some 100 yards further west, by agreement with the local authorities, and crossed the wall near the present lodge. The stile has vanished but the right of way remains. Before the church at Ambleside was built all the church traffic travelled to Grasmere by these two roads for services, marriages, christenings and funerals. The present Rydal road did not then exist.

Below the river Stock in North road, the

present Ambleside was in the parish of Windermere. Its church traffic went in an opposite direction all the way to St. Martins, Bowness. On
the Grasmere side, that is, " above Stock," the
Church Path was met by a track which struck
across the valley and, by a ford over the Rothay,
it joined the Clappersgate - Fox How pack-horse
road leading to Pelter Bridge and Grasmere.

Harriet Martineau in her " Guide " writing in
1855 described the Nook Farm and Scandale Beck.
She says the traveller " must cross the bridge
and follow the cart road which brings him at
once upon the fells." She also refers to the way
up Fairfield by " Low Scandale " that is " Low
Sweden " or Nook End Bridge, it bears all these
names. *Murray's Guide* also, of 1889, shows
in its map very clearly, the road on the Rydal
side of the Scandale burn going from the bridge
almost straight up the hill and then turning west
a little and taking a line higher than the high
fall on Rydal beck. The map also shows the road
going up Rydal beck beyond the high fall towards
Fairfield. It shows too the well - known Nab
Scar track and the ancient continuation of the
Low Sweden Bridge and Grasmere Road which,
now in a most neglected state, passes the walls

of Rydal Mount and on to White Moss. - Jenkinson also, writing in 1873, in his map clearly shows the road running north from the bridge parallel with Scandale Beck and continuing in a track towards Fairfield.

The course of the Scandale Beck was altered some years ago. It originally took a line higher up on the fell towards Rydal.

In 1621 Miss Armit says the cloth trade was an important one to Ambleside district. On the Stock there were at least five mills, three for fulling and one for corn. There was also a paper mill which was turned by the Stock. The planting below Nook End Farm still bears the name of Paper Mill Coppice.

At the Knoll, Harriet Martineau's old home, there is another ancient right of way with a ford over the Rothay. The white swing gate which crosses this road is marked " Private " but it is shown in all the maps I know as a track.

Farther on there is the well-known " Stonny Lonny," that is, Stony Loanin' — the stony field, not Stony Lane as is assumed. This delightful track crosses the Rothay at Miller Bridge. It is in no danger of being lost to the public.

MOUNTAIN GLORY—RYDAL FELLS.

In view of the enormous increase of motor traffic on Lakeland roads and the discomfort and danger it causes to foot passengers, the importance of preserving such by-roads as these, and especially the ancient alternative road from Nook End Bridge by Rydal Hall and Rydal Mount to White Moss and Grasmere, cannot be exaggerated.

In his interesting little book on *Wells, Trees, and Travel Tracks* Mr. George Middleton of Ambleside says, these ancient roads often run at a moderate height along the hillsides and cut through passes, but some boldly cross over the fell sides. He goes on to make the interesting suggestion that roads of this type which mount the hills and are known as " Roman roads " are of far greater antiquity than the Roman period, being in fact " the veritable paths of the home-landers." Taking the character of the ground into account Mr. Middleton says, and I believe he is right, " the Romans were well pleased with the existing tracks and used them."

On some of them, he adds, remains of Roman work can be found, " for, doubtless the Romans would improve them and strengthen or rebuild the watch-towers or stations along their route."

Mr. Middleton thinks that the only road of

purely Roman origin in the neighbourhood is that over High Street mountain. It has a paved way of 20 feet wide and was, he suggests, intended as a link between garrison and garrison. Winter experience would, as he says, " prove this road to be more ambitious than serviceable."

I believe Mr. Middleton is right ; of course in hilly districts the roads were seldom made down in the bottom of the glens before the nineteenth century because the valleys were so wet, and for the same reason the strath or flat land surrounding the rivers in the valleys was not cultivated in those days. The cultivation was on the sides of the hills above. This custom was universal in Scotland, and the marks of the old cultivation can still everywhere be seen. It was not till the latter half of the eighteenth century that drainage commenced and the rich, sheltered, wet straths were cultivated.

The Kirkstone Pass Old Road

The old pack-horse road through the Kirkstone Pass is probably one of the most ancient in the district. By it, chiefly, my countrymen came from the other side of Tweed when they set out to " drive ta cattle "—other people's. This old road was the thoroughfare, the historic highway from the north. From Ambleside the Westmorland men used to hurry to stop the foe if possible, before they descended into the more fruitful fields on Windermere side and in the Rothay and Brathay valleys.

In the Kirkstone Valley this track may still be seen on the north side of the road, near the ruins of the old Smiddy attached to the mines which were once worked at the spot.

This track is in a good state of preservation and is still in use all the way down to Hartsop Hall where it went through the passage which has now been roofed over to form the entrance hall of the reconstructed house. The story is told, and I believe it is true, that one day a horseman rode up to the new door of what is now the entrance hall, and demanded admittance so that he might ride through. No new-fangled road, he claimed, could deprive the public of this ancient right of way. It ended amicably by his riding through as was his right. The road is continued at the back and, under splendid trees, above the shores of Brothers Water, takes you down to Hartsop Bridge ; a very lovely road it is.

CHAPTER XIII

IN PRAISE OF HUSBANDRY

What toil can give such sights and sounds as ours ?
  What craft such gracious memories doth yield—
The call of lowing herds when homeward bound,
  Wading knee-deep amongst the clover flowers,
The laverock hovering o'er the mellow field.

Some picture fills each day the whole year round,
  For those who labour in the earth's demesne ;
Sights that can ravish sense—and sweeter sound ;
  Scents of lush grass and languorous meadow-queen.

MACKENZIE MACBRIDE.

THE famous Rydal valley follows the windings of
the river Rothay from Grasmere to Ambleside and
includes the fine pass between Nab Scar of the
Fairfield range, and Lanty Scar and Loughrigg.
Below the fells lies some of the best agricultural
land in Westmorland, rich cornfields and pastures
and splendid woodlands. Around it are some of
the most romantic of the Lakeland mountains,

hills remarkable for their noble outlines. They form quite the finest group I know in England, and Nature in the Rothay Valley has spread the richest garlands at their feet. The Valley is a continuation of the great gap that contains Windermere Lake itself. From it nearly all the highest of the Lakeland hills can be seen.

Nowhere else in northern England can we find the same wealth of verdure, of flowers, wild and cultivated. The yellow stonecrop invades even the bare stone walls, and hangs down in loops and festoons a foot deep along the roads. Around even the hard stony hills show patches of bracken, bleached by autumn to a pale pink. The tall fir trees stand up in sharp contrast to the fells, with their dark leaves and rose-madder stems ; in early spring the larch tree, hardy and quick in growth, and the only one of the pine family that casts its foliage, opens out afresh in golden-yellow splendour. Wordsworth opposed its introduction as a vulgar newcomer, but no one can deny that it lends a new and rich beauty to the becks and burns that flow down from the sides of the mountains whose dark forms shut in this paradise.

Fairfield rears his long and graceful front

sheltering the Rydal Glen from the north-east, towering to 2863 feet and joining hands with Helvellyn. Nab Scar lies west of it and its cone-topped fellows, Heron Pike, Great Rigg and Lord Crag run out at an angle from Fairfield's great rampart. On the west side of the valley opposite, Lanty Scar an offshoot of Loughrigg (the long hill that fills up the space from Water-head to Grasmere) runs picturesquely out into this Rydal, Ambleside, Grasmere Valley. To the north - west lie the Sergeantman, Greenup Edge the imposing mass of the Langdale Pikes, Bowfell, and Crinkle Crags. All these mountains are bare and bleak, and all the hills to the east are bleak and bare also ; the Ambleside valley lies like a very jewel in their midst. The south end of Windermere is tamer though rich and pastoral, and Derwentwater is perhaps more beautiful but it has nothing to compare with the wonderful scenery at the northern head of its great rival.

CHAPTER XIV

AMBLESIDE AND TROUTBECK PRIVILEGES

MR. GEORGE GATEY in an article " How Customary Tenure was established in Westmorland," some years ago pointed out that in that county farms were held on condition of providing men to take the field against the Scots for a limit of forty days in the year. If I remember rightly these tenants paid the usual two years' rent on change of tenant by death or alienation but in Ambleside and Troutbeck they only paid one year's rent on change of lord and two years' rent on change of tenant.

Mr. Gatey suggested that the reason why Ambleside and Troutbeck paid less was that when the Scots made their forays on horseback there were only two passes reasonably accessible by which they could raid the lands of lower

Westmorland — Dunmail Pass and Kirkstone Pass. This latter road was the easiest to attack and the onerous duty of defending it fell on the tenants of Ambleside and Troutbeck. The country estates of Westmorland were, Mr. Gatey adds, " from their very origin freehold " . . . and the tenure was " of the most honourable sort —by military service."

By this "customary" tenure a widow is entitled to the whole of the profits of the estate for life. In freehold tenure the widow is only entitled to one-third of the profits.

James VI. and the Statesmen

An attempt was made by James VI. when he succeeded to the English throne to treat the Statesmen as mere tenants at will. The Statesmen rebelled and the matter went after James's death before the Court of Star Chamber who in 1625 confirmed the Statesmen's lands in perpetuity as held *in capita*, that is direct from the Crown.

In 1794, according to the Agricultural Survey, about two-thirds of the county of Cumberland was held by these " Estatesmen " in holdings

A FARMSTEAD, LITTLE LANGDALE.

of the value of from £15 to £30 rental. Most of these were bought up later by the big landowners, a fact which has been greatly deplored by many, both for sentimental reasons and for those of public economy. It followed that men in the Lake District, as in Scotland, have everywhere given place to sheep or game. The consequence was that when the enemy came and foreign supplies were stopped we went short of bread and potatoes and oatmeal and other crops.

The Statesmen filled also another important function, they governed themselves and showed their interest in education when any opportunity offered, as will be seen from Adam Walker's account of Auld Hoggart's Plays at Troutbeck which I quote in another chapter.

A small sum, one or two pence, was paid by the Statesmen to the lord of the manor, but as Miss Armit points out taking Ambleside as an example, the statesmen Braithwaites, Forresters, Newtons, Jacksons and the tradesmen ruled while the lord of the manor had little or nothing to do with the town.

CHAPTER XV

OLD WESTMORLAND HOUSES

IN the old farm-houses such as those on Chapel Hill, Ambleside, at Little Langdale and in the Troutbeck valley—of rare beauty and interest, a spinning gallery was added and some of these may still be seen, perhaps the most beautiful of them being at the village last named. There is a strong tendency, however, to remove all these charming old houses. What we want is a first-rate architect to come forward with a plan for heightening the ceilings without interfering with the structure, as the rooms in the older houses are often so low that a man of 5 feet 5 inches may knock his head on entering, against a great oak beam. This difficulty could I suggest be met by deepening the foundation and putting in a concrete floor. This with a layer of tar or pitch over the concrete could be covered with boards. With proper ventilation this would be perfectly dry—drier than the present earth and flag floors, and would save these, often roomy old places, to charm future generations.

The old houses with the small windows and tremendously thick walls were most of them built in the seventeenth century to keep the Scots out. Before about the middle of that century, the farm-houses and statesmen's houses generally, on both sides of the Border, were made of wood and mud and were practically fireproof.

The stone peels and castles were built by the wealthier landowners.

Among the best specimens of the old States-men's house I know is the farm-house of Glencoin near Stybarrow on Ullswater, and the house of the Walmsley family on Chapel Hill, Ambleside. The latter, I think I have been able to prove, belonged formerly to the old and well - to - do family of Forrester, the main branch of which died out about 1730. The house was bought by the grandmother of the present owners. The place is in splendid repair and the oat-bread press with the initials of the Forresters is still preserved, an excellent example of the old wood - carving in which the Westmorland folk excelled. The

Westmorland man's lack of romance and of historical background, also his lack of folk-songs as compared with the tremendous mass possessed by the Borderer, have been referred to by many writers including some of the best like Mr. Herman Prior long ago, and Mr. A. G. Bradley, but I suggest that in this art of carving wood the Westmerian found himself—and could, with a training in ornament—do excellent work.

The ornament used on the presses and coffers and oat - bread presses is very mixed. It has generally some few local survivals of Keltic work, but is in the main of Renaissance date and origin.

CHAPTER XVI

AN OLD COUNTY TOWN

HAWKSHEAD AND ITS ANCIENT STREETS

> Oh ! pleasant, pleasant were the days,
> The time when in our childish plays,
> My sister Emmeline and I
> Together chased the butterfly !
> A very hunter did I rush
> Upon the prey :—with leaps and springs
> I followed on from brake to bush,
> But she, God love her ! feared to brush
> The dust from off its wings.
>
> WORDSWORTH.

HAWKSHEAD is not quite an old county town but it is next door to being one, for it was the legal and administrative centre of the ancient district of Furness long before big towns like Barrow were thought of. There the Abbot of Furness and his Bailiff held their Manor Courts in the old hall which stands a little to the side of the main road from Ambleside. In this old collegiate or Court-house, now used as a farm, the monks of Furness stayed who ministered at the splendid old church of St. Michael which stands on the hill at the other end of the village.

It is of great interest and worth an afternoon to itself, for it has not been converted into a vulgar brand-new looking building, by means of what used to be called churchwarden's Gothic additions and improvements. I should have much liked to have seen the interior in detail, but, though I found the door open as every church door should be, my companion was waiting in the lane below. For, not daring to ask him to see the church, I had given him the slip and, knowing he had a legal mind and had come out for one object—the walk itself, I only spent time enough to catch the antique spirit of the place, to note the tomb of the knightly family of Sandys, to realise the sense of comfort and lack of stiffness in this the people's church, and to admire the fine columns and other striking features of the building.

I joined my friend Aramis, who has many of D'Artagnan's fighting qualities ; he reminded me that the wind was cold and he had not known where I had got to.

Wordsworth's School

However, he consented to walk up to the old Free Grammar School where Wordsworth and his brother, who by the way became Headmaster of Trinity, went as boys. The school was founded by one of the same Sandys family, who was Archbishop of York, in 1658.

My friend Aramis knew the town intimately and walked through it with precision, very much as though he had been taking an inventory for a client. However, even a deliberate man does not need to make a long stay in Hawkshead to discover its quaint courts and squares filled with white cottages joining one another, and note the adoption of narrow entrances as was done so notably in Penrith, Alston and Kendal. As in these places, in fact, the houses and the whole town, were built with the aim of making rallying-points which could be held by small numbers of Hawkshead men. This on days when Galloway nags and Highland ponies that could speed up the steepest fell, brought their masters, men of many songs and much chaff, to lift the cattle and such gear as could be placed cannily on a pony's back—and what could not be ?

On those occasions, all the young ne'er-dae-weels who had been breaking other folk's heads, or stealing other folk's beasties, or who had turbulent mothers-in-law, slid out of the town, as the invaders were leaving in the mirk, and joined in among the blue bonnets behind the pipers. For it was well known that most sacred of all things to a Scot was the law of hospitality and that a Scottish host fought for his guest. So it was that, despite the repeated protests made by the kings of England, against the harbouring by the Scots of Englishmen who were " wanted," the refugee was safe.

Again it was some advantage to these men that in Scotland you could be hanged only for some twenty offences while under English law you could be hanged for over a hundred! There was thus, for business men like these, much more scope in Scotland, and for the hangman much less.

HAWKSHEAD.

CHAPTER XVII

ESTHWAITE WATER

AND THE WAY BACK

YES, if Lakeland visitors want to see a most
delightful specimen of an ancient Border town
they should find Aramis and get him to take
them to Hawkshead. If they go without him
they will never be able to break away from its
charm and enchantments, but Aramis being of
legal leanings has no compunction and will take
them home.

It should be known that Hawkshead had a
great and busy hiring fair, and at one time had
yet another claim to importance; it was the
centre in this now lonely region for the sale of
woollen yarns and woollen garments. In all
the farms and houses and cottages in the north,
the spinning-wheel was kept going, spinning the
wool from the local flocks of sheep, and the West-

morland farmers, like the Lowland and Highland farmers, were clad entirely with cloth and woollen garments made in their own homes.

But I have not quite done. Before we leave Hawkshead we must take a peep at Esthwaite the only quiet-going, gentleman's park kind of lake in this district.

It has none of the wild gipsy loveliness of Blea, or Angle or Grisedale tarn, but there is a beauty of the noon as well as of the scarlet dawn and the flaming gold-red sunset. Esthwaite and Elter-water, and the tame southern end of Windermere, have that more sober mid-day beauty.

From the road from Hawkshead to Ambleside we get a much finer series of views than when journeying to Hawkshead. On the right as we leave the town we have the Colthouse heights, and beyond them, the Claife Heights above Winder-mere ; to the west we have Hawkshead moor and Coniston Moor beyond. At Colthouse, by the way, there is an old quaker church and burial-ground of much interest.

When we reach the hamlet of Outgate we begin to get far finer views at each turn of the road. Seen from this side of the lake Wansfell has a new dignity and is hardly recognisable for that reason.

Of Fairfield we have a magnificent view and also of his satellite Hart Crag. Red Screes towers up to the right of these graceful giants like a huge lump, with Woundle Fell in the centre, and opposite, on the right is the always graceful outline of Ill Bell.

On the other side, a little nearer, is Snarker Pike, which also offers a much sharper, finer, cone-like outline than that we see from the Ambleside neighbourhood, as do his neighbours High and Low Pikes. In fact all the summits to the north-east show us their peaks which are all at their south-west end and stand grandly over the wonderfully beautiful Ambleside and Rydal Valley.

The Hawkshead road stands opposite the centre of these most graceful of Westmorland's mountains. As the land in front of us slopes down towards Windermere the result is that from no other road I know can we get a view of these giant hills so complete, so varied and so unobstructed.

From Hawkshead there is a splendid walk southward by the shores of Windermere and the woods of Furness to the Ferry Inn where we can cross to Bowness and get a coach to Windermere village or Ambleside.

CHAPTER XVIII

GRASMERE OF THE GARDENS·

I know a garden, free and fair,
And no neat hedge nor trim parterre
Vexes the idle spirit there :

No order doth those paths oppress !
As wayward as a wandering tress,
Round as a loving arm's caress ;

No prim lawn tells within its nooks
Of diligence with virtuous looks,
And lessons learnt in copy-books ;

Few tasks, indeed, for spade or shear
Present themselves throughout the year ;
Only the birds are busy here.

Neglect at leisure ; leave at will ;
Bury your talents ; doze your fill—
The gold of fate you cannot spill :

For here the hop vine's tendrils fall
In tumbled splendour over all,
And brackens fence the southern wall.

The rowan throws a tender spray
To his lady love across the way,
And looks into her eyes all day.

And by the May-tree yonder, grows
The flower the Persian maiden knows ;[1]
Fit even to match our Western rose !

Yet 'mongst the weeds, that vagrant band,
A few rare plants neglected stand,
Set by a vanished lady's hand.

Thus even here, where all seems glad,
And in romantic raiment clad,
The thoughts come stealing strange and sad ;

For it is like the world indeed—
The rare plant hidden by the weed ;
Choked by its foolish strife and greed !

MacKenzie MacBride.

GRASMERE is well known as a climbing centre but it is more than that, it is of all the Lake District villages richest in gardens and flowers. The magnificent gardens of Lake Road, Windermere, are show places and from them we can get one of the finest views of the splendid Crinkle Crags and Bowfell group, but Grasmere is a homely spot and she wears her flowers naturally as the May Queen's garlands are worn by a

[1] The lilac

country maid. Grasmere charms you with its simplicity as well as by its beauty. The village—we can call Grasmere a village without offending the villager—is also more local than modernised Windermere and ambitious Ambleside. At Grasmere great service has been done to keep the Westmorland dialect in Westmorland, where it should be, by the annual dialect play. All the parts are taken by natives but the plays were started over thirty years ago by a Scotswoman Miss Caroline Fletcher. No one but a Scot would have shown so much appreciation of other folk's good things! In old times we appreciated their cattle, to‑day we appreciate their dialect! Miss Fletcher for many years wrote the plays herself while her father was Rector of the Parish. She is still keenly interested in them and I had the distinction of sitting beside her at the play of last winter and it was only by turning the conversation on to the Scots dialect that I discovered who she was. " Yes I understand it " (the play), I replied in answer to a question, " quite well—it is like Braid Scots with the music left out." " Ah yes," she replied promptly, " I love the Broad Scots the best of all."

" Then you must be Miss Fletcher," I said.

" Your dialect play idea is a splendid one, I wish other districts would take it up."

Besides its play Grasmere is noted for its Rushbearing ceremony on St. Oswald's Day—the very prettiest procession I have ever seen. The custom is also upheld at Ambleside, Great Musgrave and Warcop on old Midsummer Day. It used to be common also in many parts of Lancashire.

Grasmere's Saint who resembled the Kaiser

St. Oswald is the name of Grasmere's charming old church. Did Oswald deserve this high compliment of being the saint to whom the church that fits best its surroundings in all Lakeland is dedicated ? King Oswald it was who, a century after the English of the Kingdom of Northumbria had been taught Christianity by the Scots monks of Iona and Lindisfarne, attempted to " convert " and conquer the Mercians.

Oswald had been sheltered when in trouble by Scotland and was converted, and baptized at Iona. He was very keen on the new religion but when he was able to recapture his father's throne he tried to make the best of both worlds by seizing the territory of his fellow-Christians the Welsh.

With this kind of religious fervour the Kaiser made us fairly familiar in the late War and indeed, in a lesser form it has not been unknown to us British and to our French neighbours when dealing with " savages." In this case the Welsh were by far more civilised than Oswald and his barbarians. Well, like " Weelyam " of Prussia, Oswald found very tough customers among the gallant Welsh chieftains, and found also a veritable Napoleon in leadership and in statesmanship in Penda, king of Mercia, which was then a very small nation. Indeed Penda, though a heathen, seems to have been really a far juster, better and more " Christian " man than Oswald. For Penda left the Welsh to choose their own religion and formed a kind of league with them and others to resist the greedy Northumbrian kings.

Oswald they defeated and killed at Maserfield in 642. They carried on the great fight for thirty years and the Welsh were able to preserve those sacred things—their identity, their mother tongue, and the landmarks of their fathers, through the help of this old " heathen " who, fourteen hundred years ago, stood up for " self-determination " and religious liberty.

STICKLE TARN, LANGDALE.

Village Industries

If Grasmere's Saint fails lamentably to withstand honest criticism, Grasmere herself deserves praise for her efforts to develop village industries, and so to save Lakeland workers from the tainted air of factories and towns. The exhibition held at Grasmere last summer which was open to all comers, was an admirable one and set visitors enquiring for village-made cups and saucers from Hartsop; brass-work from Morecambe and Keswick and needle-work from all the villages.

CHAPTER XIX

EASDALE TARN

FROM the Grasmere road, opposite to Miss Reed's bookshop, there is a road which starts from the main, Dunmail Rais road at a right angle and goes on to Easdale Tarn.

By this road we reach one of the most charming spots in charming Grasmere. In five minutes we are beside a burn whose brown water, hurrying over silver-grey stones, is to-day crossed by shafts of golden sunlight, and gold and brown make always a lovely contrast. The famous Goody Bridge passed, and we are out in the open, and there on the opposite side are the hills bright red with bracken. Over them is that indescribable, unpaintable smoke-blue haze which haunts these glens. Here we have again, the contrast of yellow and gold hillsides with this smoke-blue; and the dark of the firs against the mantle of rich brown

leaves at their feet with the glittering silver of
the burn below.

The scene is very Highland in character
as we follow the stream; the great boulders
are covered with gorgeous mosses and lichens—
yellow, gold, green, brown, copper, a wonderful
variety; while on the margin of the burn under
the firs, and rendered vivid by their dark tops,
is a stretch of lush green pasture.

Now as we ascend a quite easy slope to see the
waterfall, we reach a brown pool shot with silk-
like green and fringed with rich red bracken, as
though all the wealth of nature's mine had been
flung down at this spot.

With Helm Crag on our right and Silver How
on our left, we reach the fall; a small streak of
water or grey mare's tail as they would call it
further north. The scenery is wilder with every
step we take, and the whirr of the paitrick reaches
us, suggesting far-off things.

We are surrounded by the great hills —
Helvellyn to the north-east, Helm Crag above us
and, further south, Rydal Fell, Fairfield and Seat
Sandal. On the west we have Greenup Edge,
the Borrowdale Fells beyond, and the great
Langdale range to the south.

The trees are now few ; here is a lonely one on a pillar-shaped crag. The grey rocks are studded with gold and emerald moss and the great boulders lying about are splashed with moss streaked with red and palest green. There are a few savin (*Juniperus sabina*) bushes and a tree sticking out of a cleft in a crag above.

The burn above the waterfall as we ascend takes a sharper note something like what we hear on the sea coast.

. The track winds up amongst the bracken towards the lip of the basin of rock in which lies the tarn, romantically hidden away in the gap between Helm Crag and Silver How.

And now we are at the top and enter a different region again. We are right among the mountains, the smiling Grasmere valley could hardly be more different from this spot where no tree grows, not even the hardy savin bush, and where no bird sings.

And below us, when we reach the small hut where in summer time refreshments are sold, though it is closed on this autumn day, we see spread out below the eastern barrier of hills ; hills clad with the splendid red bracken, save where the crags are too bare and precipitous. But on the stoniest crags even we see sometimes the wonderful yellow-green lichen and mosses.

To the north black crags overhang the loch or tarn so that it is completely encompassed. To the south-east, looking over two lines of hills, the view is especially grand.

The tarn itself has now caught something of the rich browns and reds of the hills, and in the shadow at the foot of the lake, it reflects much of the grim blackness of the crags at its northern end.

The story is told by De Quincey, and all the Lake District writers tell it to-day, how many years ago George Green and his wife who lived in Easdale, were lost in a heavy snowstorm on their way home from Langdale. Their six children, the oldest a girl of nine, were snowed up in their Easdale cottage for some days, until the oldest girl made her way out and reached Grasmere village and the children were promptly rescued. The bodies of their father and mother were discovered on the fells by a search party after three days' labour. Easdale Tarn has known one other tragedy—a man committed suicide in its gloomy depths.

CHAPTER XX

THE nearest way to Grisedale Tarn is from the Grasmere-Keswick Road. The old track lies at the side of the house of the late Frank Bramley— that delightful artist who painted the picture of the Grasmere Rushbearing which is housed in the Public Hall of Grasmere. Bramley's studio lies at the back of the house and a good view of it can be obtained from the path.

The climb is a stiff one but the climber is well paid by the view of the splendid colouring of the hills around him—Stone Arthur on the right, clad in pale apple green and pale russets and marked by ridges as regular as those on an opened fan. A reminder this of the tremendous scraping of the glaciers as they moved downward with their burden of rocks and boulders gathered from distant regions. They moved along slowly inch by inch some twenty - five thousand years ago.

As we climb up the steep road we soon see the great, almost straight line of one of the Lakeland hills—and I always think one of the most impressive of them—the giant Fairfield. Like a great rampart is the long and almost straight line of his snow-visited summit.

Fairfield dominates the Ambleside and Rydal neighbourhood and can be seen from Windermere and from the Furness side of the Lake. Then again his power and majesty is set off so finely by the peaks of Nab Scar, Heron Pike, Great Rigg, and High and Low Pike, whose noble outlines make the head of Windermere the most beautiful sight in all Lakeland.

The view on the opposite side, of Crinkle Crags, Bowfell and Scawfell from Skelgill and from Windermere (Lake Road) may be wilder and more mystical, but it is not so lovely, so soft, so rich in strong light and shadow by contrast of dark woods, as Fairfield and his satellites. You would have to go to Argyll or Perthshire to match them.

From Bramley's house we follow the side of a delightful burn, keeping to the track on the northern side. There is a track on the southern side of the valley also, up from the small Grasmere water reservoir. As we rise the pale green grass here, as in Langdale becomes very noticeable, contrasting splendidly with the pale red bracken and the dark red moor-grass. But the pale green is the dominant note; it fills the glen with effulgent light.

Lakeland's Distinctive Charm

This wondrous brightness of light colouring seems to me the distinctive charm of the Lake District mountains. I always believed the Scottish mountains of Argyll, Perthshire, and Inverness-shire had every loveliness possible to mountain scenery. When I saw that this wondrous brightness was a common thing in English Lakeland I felt that, whatever might and majesty our " wine-red moors " as " R. L. S." called them, possessed that was not known to Lakeland hills, this effulgence was new to me— was, in fact, their own. Hitherto the most wonderful lighting I had ever seen was that of the Hebrides—the Kintyre coast notably, facing the Atlantic. In Kintyre, especially by Machri-

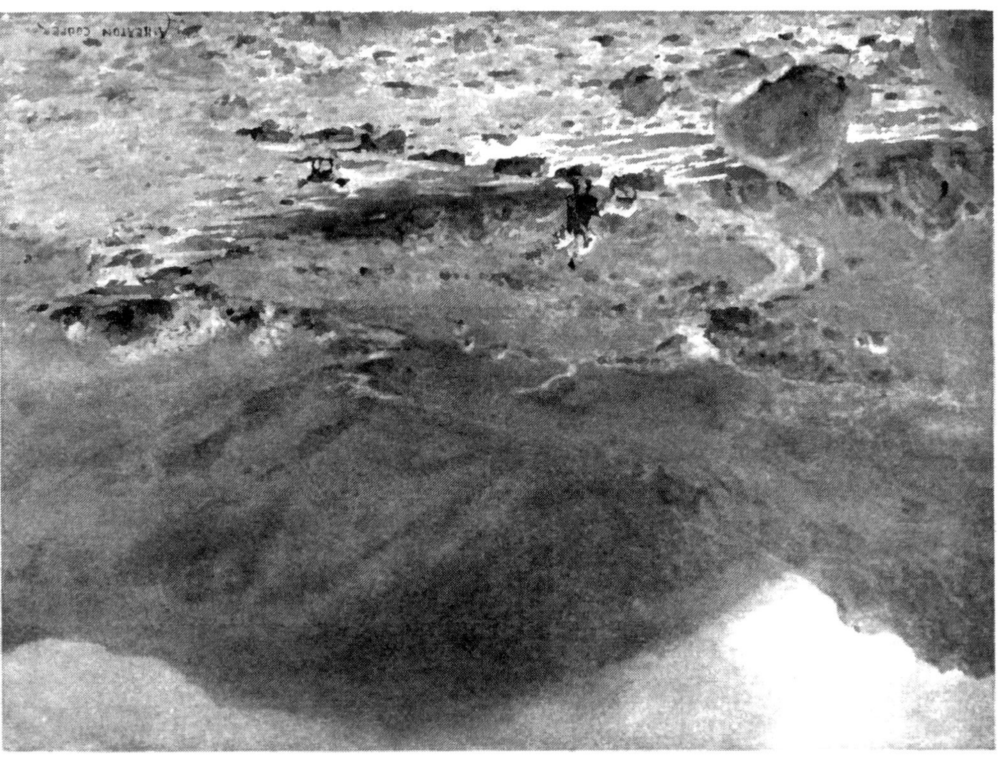

STEPPING-STONES, FAR EASDALE, GRASMERE.

hanish, Muasdale, Keil, Glen Bar, Tayinloan and Beallochruadh, the light, changeful, fleeting, iridescent, fills a common object—a rough boulder, a field of cattle, a lonely byre, farm-house, or loch, with colours rare and lovely. These it owes to the Atlantic.

Lakeland cannot give this magician's touch, but, with its pale greens and pale russets, it can fill a whole glen with splendour. In the Hebrides, though fleeting lights and the strange greens and yellows on the stones and the mosses beggar description, the hills themselves are often, after those months of gorgeous purple, dark with the dead heather. Only on the lower slopes we have the deeper russet of the decayed bracken, often mixed up with savin (juniper) and making a gorgeous contrast to it; while, on the lesser hill-tops we have the pale yellow of the bleached grass.

On the whole, however, owing to the comparative smallness of the area covered by heather, and the bleaching power of its strong sun and tremendous rainfall, Lakeland has a lighter colouring than the Hebrides.

As we rise we have an ever-increasing view of Fairfield on our right ; turning our faces westward, we get a charming glimpse of Coniston Water tucked away between the hills, and at one spot beyond Coniston and the Furness Fells we get one glimpse of the sea itself.

Again turning eastward, we reach the outlying crag which hides from us the Dollywaggon Pass, and the Helvellyn group.

We turn round this crag, and, leaving Fairfield at our back, pass through the gap, and there we have Dollywaggon Pike towering above and Little Grisedale tarn at our feet below. The soil here is very thin, and great crags, black and jagged, lower above us grimly, while the same black volcanic rocks lie around in a wild confusion as though they had been hurled from the surrounding heights.

The colouring is low, the bracken short and scarce, and the grasses bleached and not too plentiful.

The whole scene is austere and bare ; the very winds blow with a keenness that impresses one with the fact that here Nature is in her puritan mood and has closed with severity that heart so full of bounties.

The tarn fits well the romantic story attached to it for here the king of Cumbria, Domhnull, that is " Donald," after the defeat of his troops by Eadmund " the Magnificent," brother of the great King Athelstan, came in his flight and, according to the Annalists, cast into its placid waters that unlucky symbol of strife—his crown. This happened in the year 945, eight years after the great fight at Brunanburh in which Athelstan defeated King Constantin of Scotland, a very doughty warrior.

CHAPTER XXI

LAKE OF THE GOLDEN CROWN

" DUNMAIL " LAST KING OF CUMBRIA

> They now have reached that pile of stones,
> Heaped over brave King Dunmail's bones,
> He who once held supreme command,
> Last King of Rocky Cumberland ;
> His bones and those of all his power,
> Slain here in a disastrous hour.
>
> WORDSWORTH.

WHO was Dunmail ? This is the question asked by every visitor on riding or walking over that wild pass where lies at the summit the cairn or heap of stones, so famous in Lakeland, called " Dunmail Rais."

None of the guide-books satisfactorily answers this question so that the whole story has come to possess a mythical suggestion about it. One of the best guide-books says, for example, " A heap of stones on the top (*i.e.* of the pass) is said

to mark the place of an engagement between
Dunmail, king of Cumberland and Edmund the
Saxon king, in 945. The former was defeated
and killed, the eyes of his two sons were put out
by order of Edmund, and the territory was given
to Malcolm, king of Scotland."

I think it can be shown quite clearly that this
cannot be true, though "Dunmail," that is
Donald, was certainly defeated at Dunmail Rais.
The other tradition which makes him cast his
crown after the battle, into Grisedale Tarn, may
quite well be true. From the battle he escaped
to Wales and ruled there. Later he went to
Rome where he died thirty years after the famous
fight.

We are told that when the last British king
of Cumbria died Constantin II. the powerful
king of the united Picts and Scots, "was able
to get his brother, Donald, made king." I will
show that Donald was allied to the Cumbrian
royal house.

Donald was succeeded by his son Owain, who
was, with Constantin and Anlaf, defeated at the
great battle of Brunanburh in 937.

At a Congress held in A.D. 934 at Dacre Constantin, king of Scotland, and his nephew Eoghan

or " Eugenius " (which is the latinised form of Owain or Eoghan) king of Cumbria, met Athelstan and did homage to him. Mr. White mentions that there is still a room in Dacre Castle known as the room of the three kings. Owain is mentioned by William of Malmesbury as nephew of Constantin king of Scots in 934.

Thus Donald (" Dunmail ") was grand-nephew of Constantin II., and was the son of Owain not the son of Donal, as is stated by Mr. C. A. Parker in his excellent *Shelagh, Olaf Cuaran's Daughter*. Thus he was of the race of Kenneth MacAlpin who by marriage, or descent from the kings of the Northern Picts, had united the two kingdoms that made up Scotland north of the Forth and Clyde.

Edmund's quarrel with " Dunmail " was that he, as king of Cumbria, which was all that remained of Strathclyde the ancient kingdom of the Gwynedd, had sided with the Norse chiefs who had been driven out by Edmund.

Edmund was helped in his advance against the Norse by King Malcolm I. of Scotland, who was also a descendant of Kenneth MacAlpin (first king of both Picts and Scots as a united whole) and of Constantin II. After the defeat

of Donald (" Dunmail ") and the remnant of
the Norse hosts, his kingdom of Cumbria became
Malcolm's share of the spoil, the condition being
that he should be Edmund's fellow - worker by
sea and land.

The Chroniclers say the Scots " were thus
set to keep the Welsh in subjection," but this
is not very accurate, for there were Picts also in
Cumbria and some Norsemen settled there.

The gain to the English was peace and
the overlordship of the ancient kingdom of
Cumbria.

Legend tells a very different story. It was
put into ballad form by John Pagen White in
the 'sixties as follows :—

> Climb thou the rugged pass and see
> High midst those mighty mountains three,
> How in their joint embrace they hold
> The mere that hides his crown of gold.
>
> There in that lone and lofty dell
> Keeps silent watch the sentinel ;
> A thousand years his lonely rounds
> Have traced unseen that water's bounds.
>
> His challenge shocks the startled waste,
> Still answered from the hills with haste.
> As passing pilgrims come and go
> From heights above or vales below.

When waning moons have filled their year,
A stone from out that lovely mere
Down to the rocky Raise is borne,
By martial shades with spear and horn.

As crashes on the pile the stone
The echoes to the King make known
How still their faithful watch they hold
In Grisedale o'er his crown of gold.

And when the Raise has reached its sun
Again will brave King Donnll come ;
And all his warriors marching down
The dell, bear back his golden crown.

They buried on the mountain's side
King Donnll, where he fought and died.
But mount and mere and moor again
Shall see King Donnll come to reign.

Mantled and mailed repose his bones
Twelve cubits deep beneath the stones ;
But many a fathom deeper down
In Grisedale mere lies Donnll's crown.

And Donnll mantled, crowned and mailed,
Again shall Cumbria's King be hailed ;
And o'er his hills and valleys reign
When Eildon's heights are field and plain.

I have ventured in quoting these verses to
spell " Dunmail " in a way which is nearer the
actual sound. By doing so the confusion with
the word " mailed," twice used in the poem,
is also avoided and the accent falls on the first

GRISEDALE TARN (ULLSWATER IN THE DISTANCE).

syllable " Don " as is needed for the verse, instead of falling on " mail " as it is wrongly made to do in English.

The word " Rais " was quite commonly used for a castle or tower or other building as in " Stewart's Rais," the name of the old castle near Barrhead, and " Stonerais " in Northumberland which was probably built at a time when stone buildings were first coming into fashion on the Border.

DESCENT OF DUNMAIL (DONALD), KING OF CUMBRIA

(WHO WAS DEFEATED AT THE PASS OF DUNMAIL)

Line of Fergus Mor, King of Scots,
brother of Lorn (A.D. 498–501).

Alpin,
King of Scots, d. 834.

Donald IV.,
succeeded his brother Alpin 834.

Kenneth MacAlpin,
first King of Scots and of Picts,
succeeded his uncle Donald IV. 841–863.

Donald V.,
succeeded his brother Kenneth 860–863.

Cu,
married Rune,
Prince of Cumbria.

Aedh,
succeeded his brother Constantin I.,
killed 880.

Constantin I.,
succeeded his uncle Donald V. 863–879.

Donald,
brother of Constantin II.,
elected King of Cumbria.

Constantin II.,
grandson of
Kenneth MacAlpin,
succeeded his cousin
Donald VI. 900, d. 942,
reigned 45 years.

Donald VI. 889–900,
grandson of Kenneth MacAlpin.

Indulf,
grandson of Kenneth MacAlpin,
reigned 8 years.

Owain, son of Donald,
King of Cumbria.

Malcolm I.,
son of Donald VI., d. 951,
added Cumbria to Scotland.

Colin, killed 971 in Lothian,
succeeded Dubh,
reigned 5 years.

DUNMAIL, *i.e.* Donald,
King of Cumbria,
defeated at Dunmail Rais
in 945 by Edmund;
died 30 years later.

2. Kenneth II., succeeded Colin,

Malcolm II., conquered Lothian,
added it to Scotia (1004–1034).

dau. Bethog, m. Crinan.

Duncan I., King of Cumberland,
killed by MacBeth (see page 107).

1. Dubh, succeeded Indulf, d. 967,
reigned 5 years.

Kenneth III., son of Dubh,
killed by Malcolm II.

Lulach, 1078, son of Kenneth III.
and stepson of MacBeth, his guardian.

CHAPTER XXII

DUNCAN, KING OF CUMBERLAND

WHY HE WAS SLAIN BY MACBETH

IT will be seen from the pedigree above that by the ancient Scottish law, the brothers of the king succeeded him first, then his sons and their cousins. Only an adult could rule. When a king was crowned his Tanist or successor was also chosen. A king was deposed for any failure in courage or honour, or defect of mind or person. That is, if he lost an eye or a limb. Hence Edmund is said to have put out the eyes of Dunmail's sons to ensure against their succession.

The law as to the succession of brothers was certainly in every way excellent. It secured as king, generally speaking, a full-grown man who had acted as assistant king (Tanist), and it saved the country from the thing which brought disaster to Scotland after the unhappy adoption or part adoption, of the feudal system—minorities.

Under the old Keltic system (Scottish and Irish) every man carried a marshal's baton in his sporran as it were. Every man could rise from the ranks. There were no poor, the land belonged to the clan—not to the king, or to a handful of foreigners as it did later under feudalism.

No wonder that the Pictish nation was so strong and rule so settled that men often reigned for twenty and thirty and forty years. No wonder that when their kinsmen, the Scots, came with newer ideas, more advanced art and scholarship, they listened to them and accepted. No wonder that in the days of those vigorous early kings the Kenneths, Malcolms, the Alexanders, and of David and the early Stuarts, Scotland was a most flourishing land in the very districts where we now have a desert and a wilderness.

From the pedigrees [1] it will also be seen that Shakespeare in his immortal tragedy put his money on the wrong horse as it were. Malcolm II. a great king and soldier, saw that the feudal system was spreading, and broke the Keltic law by putting forward as his successor the king

----

[1] See pages 98 and 107.

of Cumberland (or rather, of all Strathclyde) his grandson Duncan I., who bears in the play the fine title of " the Gentle Duncan." Thus the wrongdoer was not MacBeth who was supporting as he was bound to do, the claims of Lulach his stepson, grandson of King Kenneth III. (997–1004) son of Duff, son of Malcolm I.

In the reign of Henry III. (1263) an agreement
was made between the Abbot of Shap and Gilbert
de Berebrunne or Barebon (brother of Sir Richard
de Barbon of Barbon, Westmorland) and William
de Lascelles and Joan and Amice their wives and
Agnes, sister of Joan and Amice, concerning
land in Renegill which Roland de Rosgill, their
father, had formerly held.   Among the witnesses
were Sir Patrick and Sir Matthew de Rosgill,
knights, Thomas de Hastings, Master Walter de
Ravensby and others.

The point is that Joan and Amice de Rosgill were great-granddaughters of Gospatrick's
daughter Gunnilda who married Orm great-
grandson of Ivo de Tallebois,[1] Baron of Kendal,
brother of the Count of Anjou.   To Orm,
Waltheof, his brother-in-law, gave with his sister,
the Cumberland estates of Seaton, Camberton,
Flemingby and Crocksothen.

It has been stated that Cristiana, " widow of
Thomas Lascels," married Robert Bruce the
competitor for the Scottish crown.   King Robert
Bruce's own mother was Devorgilla of Galloway.

In the same century Thomas de Culwen

---

[1] *Kingsley took his fancy portrait of this man from the discredited
Chronicle of Ingulphus of Croydon and Peter of Blois.*

STYHEAD GILL (BORROWDALE TO WASTWATER).

great-great-grandson of Orm, married Joan de Lascels.

Before 1344 Lascells of Escryk in Yorkshire made an alliance with the heiress of the other branch of the Westmorland family of de Barbon who had held the manor of Barbon for some two hundred years and the Barbon estate passed to Lascells. This Barbon was a descendant of Sir Richard, elder brother of Gilbert de Barbon who married Joan de Rosgill. Gilbert's immediate descendants held land in Yorkshire ; and William de Berburn held land, probably from the Priory, at Warmington in Warwickshire in 1327, when the king had made Thomas de Multon head of the French monks there owing to the war with France. De Multon was also a descendant of Gospatrick. Thomas Barbon later held land at Whitacre. Dr. Brabourne, secretary to Bishop Juxon who attended Charles I. in the last tragic scene, came from the same branch of the Westmorland stock, which is represented by the descendants of Butler Greatrex (of Anchorage) who was Commandant at Cuxhaven during the French wars. His adventures were told in the novel *Maurice Drummore : the Memoranda of a Marine Officer*, a brilliant and amusing book which Sir W. Robertson Nicoll stated he had read fifty times.

In Westmorland cadets of the senior branch—the Barbons or Brabins of Docker and Whittington Halls, are represented by the North family, of Newton Hall, one of whom married the heiress, many years since ; and the Casterton property of another very old cadet of de Barbon, passed by marriage, to the branch of the Curwens of Workington from whom sprang the great antiquary Camden. Their property, if I remember rightly, went later by marriage to the Nicholsons.

The descent of Lascelles and connection with Westmorland families is shown in the pedigree attached.

DESCENT OF LASCELLES

FROM

KENNETH MACALPIN AND ALFRED THE GREAT

Bethog (daughter of Malcolm II., king of Scotland), sixth in descent from Kenneth MacAlpin. = Crinan, Lay Abbot of Dunkeld, head of the Scottish Church ; Seneschal of the Isles : Lord of Athol.

1. Duncan I., King of Strathclyde, later King of Scots, m. daughter or sister of Siward Digera, Earl of Northumberland, defeated and killed by MacBeth 1034.

2. Maldred, m. Ealgyth, daughter of Earl Uchtred by his 3rd wife, daughter of Ethelred II. of England and sixth in descent from Alfred the Great.

Malcolm III. (Canmore), King of Scots 1057, son of Duncan I. = 1. Ingeborg. 2. St. Margaret.

1. Gospatrick I., Earl of Northumberland, later Earl of Dunbar, seventh in descent from Alfred.

2. Maldred II.

Duncan II., King of Scots, eldest son of Malcolm Canmore, 1094. = 2. Etheldreda, married her cousin Duncan II., King of Scots.
3. Gospatrick II., Earl of Dunbar.
4. Waldeve,

1. Gunnilda, m. Orm, great-grandson of Ivo de Tallebois, Baron of Kendal, lord of Windermere, Grasmere, Ambleside, Rydal, etc., ancestor of the Bruces of Skelton and of Queen Catherine Parr, wife of Henry VIII.

William, m. Alice de Romelli, daughter of William le Meschen.

Cristiana, m. (1) Duncan de Lasceles.

"The Boy of Egremont," grandson of Duncan II.

1. Gospatrick, ancestor of de Culwen of Workington.
2. Robert, ancestor of (1) Joan de Rosgill, who married Gilbert, brother of Sir Rd. de Barbon of Barbon, Westmorland, before A.D. 1263 and
(2) Ancestor of Amice de Rosgill, younger sister of Joan, who married before 1263, William de Lasceles.

CHAPTER XXIV

THIRLMERE AND BLENCATHARA

With toil the King his way pursued
By lovely Threlkeld's waste and wood,
Till on his course obliquely shone
The narrow valley of St. John,
Down sloping to the western sky,
Where lingering sunbeams love to lie.
Scott's *Bridal of Triermain.*

KESWICK is one of the most easily approached of the Lake District towns, and one of the best centres for those who would see the great hills on the north edge of the mountain district and also on the western edge. Unlike Ambleside and Grasmere, which would be ruined by a railway running through that marvellous Winder-mere-Ambleside-Rydal-Grasmere string of valleys, Keswick has a plain side to her face. She smiles only on one cheek, and the railway line from Penrith comes along that side by the compara-tively humble region of Penruddock and Threlkeld, which lies at the foot of the splendid hill with the Welsh-Keltic name Blencathara. True it has been vulgarised in a language far inferior in sonorous sounds, far less appreciative of poetic fitness into Saddleback—think of the anti-climax !

Blencathara—that is the tongue - shaped hill of the fort, not of the saddle.[1] Though there are higher hills it is not surpassed in the matter of its splendid presence anywhere in the district, not even by Bowfell or Crinkle Crags, Great Gable, or the Scawfell giants.

But we must not forget that when we have passed through the Windermere to Grasmere valleys and have reached Dunmail Rais, there is still a wonderful feast in store for us on our way to Keswick because we have not only a series of views of Blencathara on many of his fronts but we have one of the loveliest and quite the highest of the English lakes to pass.

It was of course, a monstrous exaggeration to say that the damming up of lovely Thirlmere by the Manchester Corporation to obtain water for their citizens, did not destroy any of the beauty of the lake. The truth is the great bare, plain,

---

[1] *Cathar pronounced Cach-ır in Gaelic and with the " th " sound in Welsh Cathir.*

stone dam at the northern end ruins that part of Thirlmere.

As I never saw the wooden bridge that was once thrown over the Lake, nor the hamlet they submerged, I cannot say how much the aspect of the place has been changed, but even with the damage done, Thirlmere seems to me to be a marvel of beauty and its very aloofness, its silence, removes it out of the same category as Ullswater or Windermere. It belongs wholly to the mountains and its setting is as lovely as its own shores. Above it rises the great wall of Helvellyn and across the lake are Armboth and the wild Fells. To see Thirlmere however, we need to drive or walk back by the road on its western side for, fine though the glimpses of it from the Helvellyn side are, the views from the western side are incomparably finer. Wood and water, and brown fell and distant hills we have; and the rugged walls of Helvellyn, the bleak pass of Dunmail and the Borrowdale Fells, which overhang the lake. On the western side, too, the fells throw out from their group the lion-like Raven Crag with its scarred head and serrated back and its feet projecting far into the water— altogether a tremendous monster. And all along the banks lie gigantic boulders torn from it by storms, though these are now partly under water like the bridge and the house which stood below. All these things we have about us. The great things on the rest of the road are the many glimpses of Blencathara. Memories are awakened at Triermain where in his *Bridal of Triermain* Sir Walter Scott describes the castle near Thirlspot—

> But, midmost of the vale, a mound
> Arose with airy turrets crowned,
> Buttress, and rampire's circling-bound,
>   And mighty keep and tower;
> Seemed some primeval giant's hand
> The castle's massive walls had planned,
> A ponderous bulwark to withstand
>   Ambitious Nimrod's power.

And when at last we meet the road to St. John's Vale and Threlkeld, and we turn to the north-west round the shoulder of Blencathara, his predominating place in the landscape is taken by that other wide-spreading monster—Skiddaw and the Borrowdale Fells. Presently we get sight of Derwentwater, as we descend from these heights towards the beautiful old town of Keswick. But any one who wants to see the whole of Derwentwater can cross the fell at Armboth and make for Watendlath and Borrowdale.

CHAPTER XXV

IT would be difficult to find a more favoured town than Keswick. It lies amongst the great hills at the feet of one of the very highest of them, towering to 3054 feet. It is thus, higher than its romantically named and more magnificent neighbour, Blencathara, which boasts only 2847 feet. Skiddaw pushes out into the low country on the edge of the Bassenthwaite valley and is, therefore, here seen to great advantage from many points.

Through Keswick again runs the famed and lovely river the Greta. Though so close to the mountains and one of the best points for reaching the hills of the Scawfell group Keswick town is on a raised platform like Windermere village, as distinguished from Bowness and Ambleside. This certainly gives the advantage of light and brightness to both places, yet makes them colder when

A LOAD BEFORE THE STORM—CONISTON.

the winds blow down from the snow‑covered mountains to the north and east and west.

The town itself is very interesting and the town‑hall standing in the middle of the road gives a delightful old‑world touch to the whole place.

Keswick is lucky in another sense ; it has had generous citizens whose gifts of the land on both sides of its chief avenue have made this part of Keswick the most beautiful bit of road in the town and it will keep the country in the very centre of Keswick for all time, so that it can never be divorced from nature.

The town of Windermere lost an opportunity of buying a piece of land in its very centre like this some years ago and to‑day, as I have pointed out, Ambleside Urban Council has a great opportunity of immortalising itself by begging from the owner the pretty piece of garden lying in the centre of the town, at the back of the Queen's Hotel, and bordered by Compston Road on the other side.

Before we leave the town‑hall and the interesting shops, among them one in which the Keswick Arts and Crafts Guild show and sell their brass and other work, it should be remembered that at the town‑hall there is a model in relief of the

Lake District. It was made by Mr. Flintoft and was the labour of many years.

I have not seen it but I know the excellent model in Kendal Public Library—which, by the way, is full of good things and these are made very accessible by really sane catalogues—and I know many library catalogues that are by no means sane. Well, whenever I am puzzled to know what hill it was I saw say from Garburn Pass or any other point I go and have it out with the model at Kendal.

This reminds me that there is a library at Keswick which was left by Mr. Marshall. I believe it has been amalgamated with the Kelsick Trust Library as has been done in the case of the fine Armit Library at Ambleside, of which Mr. Herbert Bell is the librarian.

Keswick is the only Lakeland town I know in which there are old-book shops. In some of these I have seen some very good books on the district containing admirable pictures.

Lake Country Illustrators

Yes, Lakeland has been very well illustrated and it ought to be kind to artists, for men like William Green, Farington, Allon, J. B. Pyne and Ibbetson, rank among our best draughtsmen. Indeed, in black and white I do not think we will ever see their like again. None of these men were natives of the district. Less known as an illustrator was a great Lancastrian, who was a superb colourist and also a splendid black-and-white artist at a time when British art was falling back into the terribly literal, unimaginative manner which preceded Turner, Constable and other great men. I refer to Birket Foster whose splendid illustrations in my old 1879 copy of *Black's Guide* I rank amongst the best and most suggestive of the wonder, the glamour of these hills.

Look at his " Ullswater " with the fine sky-scape in which he excelled ; his " Friar's Crag," his " Coniston Lake," his " Grasmere " both unlike any other picture of these two last places. Then take his " Derwentwater from Ferry Crag," his " Ullswater from Gowbarrow," his " Honister Crag " and " Airey Force."

Green and Farington (as in his " Crummock Water ") sometimes, perhaps, overdo the thing, but in Birket Foster's pictures there is no straining, no excess of subject though it is a common fault in the others. He gives you a meal that will feed and inspire not gorge you.

CHAPTER XXVI

KESWICK and Derwentwater at one time belonged to the Ratcliffes, Earls of Derwentwater, through their marriage with the Derwentwater family. The romantic loyalty of the last earl and his brother to their kinsmen, the Stuarts, brought them both to the block one in 1715 and the younger brother, who was only a boy at that date, was cruelly pursued afterwards by the brutality of the Government of the time and was also beheaded in 1745 for a political offence committed thirty years before.

The execution of the Earl in 1715 was long remembered and the name " Derwentwater's Lights " was all over the north, still given to the aurora when I was a boy. It appears that on the day of his execution the aurora was seen in great splendour which was believed to betoken the anger of Heaven at the execution of so virtuous a man.

The estates of the family near Keswick and at Dilston and Alston Moor, also in Cumberland, were confiscated and given to Greenwich Hospital. Of these estates the Keswick property was bought by Mr. John Marshall and remains in his family.

In later times Keswick has had other celebrities and not the least of these was Robert Southey, who ranks amongst the best writers of prose in the language. In his day he was still more famous as a poet but the rhymed couplet in which he and Wordsworth and Scott wrote very long poems is to most of us too tedious to follow. But Southey was not more tedious than Wordsworth very often becomes, for instance in his " Waggoner," what could be less poetical or more prosaic :—

> And see beyond the hamlet small
> The ruined towers of Threlkeld hall,
> Lurking in a double shade
> By trees and lingering shadows made ?
> There at Blencathara's rugged feet,
> Sir Lancelot gave a safe retreat
> To noble Clifford from annoy
> Concealed the persecuted boy.

Southey's great book *The Life of Nelson*

remains one of our best biographies and though we may think less of his poetry to-day the more we know of him the more we think of him as a man. His presence for forty years in Keswick, his freedom from bumptiousness, vanity and bombast, and his generally kind and noble character, have left a fragrance behind among the fields and meadows he frequented.

He is buried in the graveyard of the ancient and historic church of Crosthwaite, half· a mile beyond the town. The name of the Church takes us back to the days when the Scottish monks from Iona, and later from Lindisfarne brought light and high ideals to the people of Cumbria, and indeed to districts much further south. St. Kentigern (or by his pet name St. Mungo) was a friend and relation of St. Columba, the patron saint of all Highlanders. Both belonged to the royal family of Dalriada, who ruled over Argyll and the Southern Hebrides and later amalgamated with the Picts their kinsmen, and ruled over all Scotland.

CHAPTER XXVII

AN OLD-TIME CHURCH

BESIDES the memorial to Southey in the grave-yard, inside the church there is a recumbent statue of him by Lough, a sculptor well known in his day. In the church is also a memorial to the Earl of Derwentwater of 1597 and his wife. The monument consists of a knight in armour and a lady. The whole is of bronze.

The church was restored in the 'seventies by Sir Gilbert Scott who, though a fine architect, restored too much in very many cases, Chester Cathedral for instance. Before the restoration of the building, it was used on week days as a meat market and the pews were converted into stalls by the butchers. Pigs were also penned in the church.

The situation amongst the fat, lush meadows with the surrounding hills, and the beautiful lanes of Applethwaite, is very fine but one would like to have seen this church of St. Mungo a little less like a fashionable church in a London suburb. Just a breath, a suggestion, one would have liked of those devoted old Keltic missionaries, and especially of Kentigern who founded the very Cathedral church to which this district five hundred years later belonged. At that time (1125) the " Inquest of David Prince of Cumberland " son of the king of Scots, was held to determine the lands belonging to the diocese of Glasgow. Crosthwaite church since the days of Gilbert Scott, has suffered other alterations if not restorations, which had not been completed when I was last in the building.

A number of ancient stones with Keltic sculpture upon them were then grouped together near the entrance and were carefully guarded, it should be said, by the late Canon Rawnsley. It seems to me, however, that these stones should have been kept *in situ* at all costs by Scott or any later " restorer." Instead of this being done, all over the country old tracery has been removed from the windows of buildings and stacked in a corner or on a refuse heap, instead of being left *in situ* and built round. In its place we

STYHEAD PASS (TO WASTWATER).

have allowed new and often hard and poor tracery to be used. For instance the only incongruous and unsatisfactory thing about Grasmere's delightful old church is the new window on the left hand as you enter the building.

From Crosthwaite we pass Greta Hall, the home of Southey, near Greta Bridge. There he lived for some forty years. After his death the house was bought by a member of the old Yorkshire family of Rothery who lived in it.

The lead pencil industry is still carried on in Keswick near which town plumbago or black lead was first discovered—at Seathwaite, which is, by the way, with Sty Head Pass the wettest place in all Britain. The mines here are now closed. After two centuries their place was taken by the more famous Borrowdale mines which are still worked.

On the Borrowdale Road along the shore of Derwentwater we pass the grandly named waterfall of Lodore. There is an approach to it at the side of the hotel. The name haunted me long before I saw the fall, but, like most people I was disappointed, for it had not more water in it than would make a decent shower-bath. Stock Gill Force at Ambleside is infinitely finer, and when

in spate the throbbing of its waters on the rocks
as they fall down in two streams from some
50 feet above, is very impressive, yet its height
is only 47 feet; less by 53 feet than that of
Lodore.

Further along Derwentwater side we enter
Borrowdale and can continue to Buttermere,
a distance of fourteen miles. Or we can cross
the pretty bridge at the hamlet of Grange.
Together they, bridge and hamlet, by the way,
make a very charming picture.

By another alternative road which enables you
to get grand views of the eastern side of the lake,
you can cross the bridge and walk back into
Keswick under Cat Bells and through the splendid
woods which were bought by the National Trust
and are open to the public for all time. From
this road, which runs over high ground, the Lake
can be seen in all its beauty and the hills on the
opposite shore.

CHAPTER XXVIII

In the Rydal and Ambleside Valley there are great numbers of birds ; the finches are perhaps the most familiar but the robin is the most friendly. At your house door as soon as he gets to know you are a member of the family he will come to your feet almost.

Indeed, in Ambleside Churchyard the sexton, Mr. Satterthwaite, who, by the way, is an authority on the Westmorland dialect, has got a little robin who watches him, from the top of a tombstone near by, while he is digging, and who will fly down the new-made grave to get a certain worm. One winter morning Mr. Satterthwaite put a few crumbs on his shoulders and the robin at once flew up and ate them off his back. In the store-house under the tower another robin makes his home and comes daily to be fed. The starling is also a favourite in the neighbourhood and is almost as tame as the robin. He can be heard imitating the crowing of the cock and the clucking of the hens when one of them has laid an egg. ' In fact, there is no sound the starling will not imitate. He will come quite near the house and from a branch in the early morning you can hear his guttural sounds so full of suggestion of peace and satisfaction. He is not exactly a singer but he has a very low and pretty note for all that. If you get the sun on him so that you can see his graceful shape and the lovely sheen on his green feathers, delicately spotted with grey, you will agree that he is almost as beautiful as the kingfisher in plumage and more graceful in shape because the head of the kingfisher is rather large for his size, while that of the starling is beautifully proportioned.

Branching off the Ambleside Glen is the equally lovely Brathay Valley with its splendid cliffs and woods and its leafy stream. At Skelwith, two miles up, I have seen the kingfisher watching for his prey. In the Ambleside-Rydal Valley I have seen the buzzard far up aloft, and wild swans in March flying far overhead.

In Scandale on the high ground I have heard either the wheat-ear or the stone-chat whose notes are similar.

CHAPTER XXIX

SOMETHING ABOUT THE SWAN

A FRIEND some time ago, suggested to me, that
the decrease in the number of trout in Lakeland
streams was not due to the depredations of
human poachers, as has been stated, but to the
fact that sea-birds have learnt to come much
further inland than formerly, and now invade
the lakes and their tributaries in great numbers.
Later a writer in a Lake District newspaper,
counted a company of birds to the number, I
think, of sixty-seven, including swans, cygnets,
and seagulls, flying over the Lake District, a
fact that seemed to support my friend's view.

The swans which frequent Windermere, including that notorious patriarch, " Bill," and
many generations of his descendants, and the
splendid birds which surround the prow of the
steamer at Bowness in summer time, are among

the Lake's most beautiful ornaments. They are so graceful, so suggestive of the purity and serenity of all that belongs to natural scenery, as contrasted with the dust, the bustle, the heat and the madness which characterise our city streets.

Much discussion has been going on, both here in Lakeland and on Thames side among anglers, as to whether swans or ducks are the chief offenders in destroying the young fishes, and, in consequence, spoiling the sport of the fishermen.

It has been contended by swan owners that the ducks and not the swans are the offenders, the swan being, if not fully qualified for membership of the Vegetarian Society, yet, at least chiefly vegetarian in his feeding.

Be that as it may, it would, from the point of view of the general public, be cheaper to sacrifice the anglers to the swans than the swans to the anglers, for the angler is, at best, a selfish animal, while the swan is by no means so.

And after all, the trout is a very insipid fish not to be compared to a Loch Fyne herring or a mackerel caught at 6 A.M. and eaten for breakfast at 8 A.M.

The question, as I have said, is by no means

confined to the Lake District. The West Highlands of Scotland in the north, and in the south the river Thames are the great homes of the British swan.

Indeed, one of the most picturesque things in connection with the decidedly picturesque London City Guilds is the fact that two of them, the Vintners and the Dyers, should have figured in history for certainly over 380 years as owners and preservers of this most beautiful of water-fowls.

"The Bells of Ouseley"

Then ye trout worshippers who revere still more wealth and lineage, look at the swan's pedigree ! The swan is what is called a " royal bird " and has been the most-cared-for of English fowls. According to the Swan Laws, which are very numerous, it alone of all English birds can be an " estray." Think how stylish that must be ! A law of Edward IV. provides further that no person other than the son of the king, not even an O.B.E., may possess a swan except he holds lands to the value of five merks. It was one of the prerogatives of the Crown that any swan found unmarked upon the seas or rivers of England belonged to the Crown, and no person was allowed to have a swan mark without he had received a grant of the privilege from the Crown. The marks were granted by the king's swan-herd, who was an important officer, holding authority over the entire kingdom. These laws are still in force, but, of course, any person can keep swans upon private lakes and unnavigable streams. On the river Thames the only persons possessing the privilege are the two companies named; to them and His Majesty the King, belong all the swans between London and Henley.

The centre of the swan neighbourhood is the old inn called "The Bells of Ouseley," a name deliciously suggestive of the sound of the great stream "lapsing along past villages," and of a lair among the reeds and rushes.   Here, and at Henley, Sunbury, Boulter's Lock, Cookham, Querry Wood, Woodburn Ferry, Bray Oak, and up many of the small backwaters in the neigh-bourhood, the birds may best be seen.

"THE SWAN VOYAGE"

The privilege of keeping swans on the Thames has been enjoyed by the Vintners and Dyers from

THE BORROWDALE YEWS.

remote times, for in the earliest written record (1509) the custom is familiarly referred to. The next record in the annals of the Vintners' Company occurs in 1609, when swan officers are referred to as having been appointed. It has always been the duty of the youngest of the three wardens of the Company to take charge of the swans, and he is thence called the " Swan Warden." His duty is to inspect the broods annually, and to direct the " swan marker." For this purpose he is called upon every year by the King's Swan-herd, or marker, to make the " swan voyage."

On the last Monday of July the King's representative meets the wardens of the two other owners, and they then, accompanied by members of the companies, and the swan herdsmen, start from Southwark Bridge on their voyage up Thames. This practice may possibly have been the origin of the name of the familiar " Old Swan " Pier and Wharf.

The object of this pleasant and romantic cruise is to pinion and mark the young cygnets, now some two months old. This last is done by cutting the owner's mark on the upper beak of each bird. The king's birds are marked with a " G," those of the Dyers' Company with one nick, and those of the Vintners with two nicks. This system of nicking gave rise to the well-known tavern sign which has been corrupted into " The Swan with Two Necks."

THE SWAN FROM A MATRIMONIAL POINT OF VIEW

There is one other point of view from which the swan deserves consideration in these days when Mr. Justice Darling has been bewailing the fact that every other man or woman you meet is now going in for divorce proceedings.

The character given by observers of the swan at home is interesting and reassuring in this age when even Cupid is being Americanised. " Handsome is as handsome does " is a good proverb, but it detracts nothing from the swan, for the " cob " (an excellent name for a bread-winner) is loyal as well as beautiful, being most attentive and faithful to the " pen," or female bird, and careful of the young. He is also courageous in defence of his ain fireside, and will chase invaders of his privacy for a mile and then offer fight, prepared like Bret Harte's " Mr. Jones, Lycurgus B.," " on rivals twenty-three to prove the marriage sanctity." The female bird's familiar name—suggestive of Penelope, the most constant of wives, is also not misapplied, for she is equally faithful and affectionate, and the birds are believed to pair for life, so may be said to possess the final mark of civilisation :—

THEY ARE MONOGAMISTS

and as they live for some fifty years, may frequently celebrate their golden weddings.

So it is at least satisfactory to know that the most honoured of water-birds is worthy of the praise of the poets of all ages, and of the pencil of our own painter, Lord Leighton, who introduced it so admirably into his " Odalisque " as if as a monogamistic protest against the manners of the seraglio.

Besides the excellent qualities which the bird actually possesses, the ancient Greeks attributed to it the power of song, the legend being that it exercised that gift especially when dying. The swan they knew belonged to the species known to us as the " whooper," which, though very similar to our " mute " swan in other respects, has, unlike it, a very musical and trumpet-like note. From the old Greek fable we have come

to call the last song of the poet the " swan song."
Again, in the ancient Irish legend, " The Fate
of the Children of Lir " (the original of Shakespeare's " King Lear ") who were changed into
swans by a wicked stepmother and doomed to
wander among the wild waters of the West
Highlands, the birds are gifted with the power
of song. An interesting parallel between the
Keltic and the Greek.

In Ireland even now no one will harm a swan
owing probably to some remembrance of this
ancient mythological story of Lir's children.

CHAPTER XXX

THE FAIRY PRINCESS

BLEA TARN AND THE LANGDALES

LIKE the Princess in the Fairy tale Blea Tarn is set high up, aloof, surrounded by difficulties for those who would approach.

The soft beauty of the scenery round Ambleside disappears at the charming hamlet of Skelwith where you turn up by Skelwith Force towards the Coniston road.

The country assumes a rougher, wilder, more austere aspect. We climb up until we reach a rather narrow road, on the right-hand side. If you happen to be a cyclist out of practice like myself, you look with some respect if not awe at the hairpin bend which forms the first turn in the road. You take it gingerly till you reach the straight piece which leads through the delightful old-world village of Little Langdale.

Langdale Post Office by the way, was once an Inn. Passing the well-built school you reach the road which runs for a time parallel with the Little Langdale Valley. Down below lies the fine tarn and the quaint Slater's bridge, with one or two very old houses opposite on the Tilberthwaite Coniston side. We soon leave this scene and come up under one of the shoulders of the great hill called Weatherlam.

The scene has now altered ; from the wild but wooded Little Langdale valley we have reached a region of bare mountains topped with black and splintered crags. The unexpected thing is that all the valley is full of light, despite the two black, jagged detached rocks which, like castles of the Arabian Nights, stand at each end of the glen, and the black upper ridge of Weatherlam which fills up all this side of the valley. The cause of this sense of light is that the bottom of the glen is covered with a close grass of a pale green, a lighter colour than that we know as sage green. A dull apple green perhaps would better describe it ; and among the grass and all around on the fell opposite, save at the top, lie great broad patches of dead bracken of a peculiarly low and delicate rose-pink colour.

The whole place is filled with the splendour of it. The sharp contrast of the slopes on which the heather has become quite black ; of the dark cliffs and of the scattered pines and yew trees near the old and solitary farm-house below, add greatly to this sense of light and warmth.

I have watched many wonderful effects among the Scottish hills but I do not remember anything like this combination of soft tones of colour in winter. Possibly the wet summer may have washed the harsher hues out of the bracken and have thus turned its russet almost to rose.

The road now runs downhill to a gate where commences a long uphill walk. The sides of the hills are here covered with juniper, called " savin "[1] in the local tongue. These bushes are a great boon from the picturesque point of view, on hills so thinly covered with soil. They add too beauty by contrast with the bleached green of the grass of which I have spoken.

At the top of the rise we reach another gate ; here we are on the summit and get a grand view of the Langdale Pikes to the north, and of the long side of Blaikrigg filling up the side of the

---

[1] *Juniperus sabina.*

valley, which now runs north-west. We have
thus completed a half-circle.

A few steps further and we see the famous
Blea Tarn lying down below us. The long crest
of Blaikrigg is streaked with snow above and with
bracken on the lower slopes, at its foot is a
beautiful wood of larch, Scotch fir and birch,
and, closing all in to the north is the giant mass
of the Langdales and the precipitous Pike o'
Blisco. We cross the grass which, like the fells,
is tinged with a lovely russet from the decayed
moss. We reach the high ground and there
below us like a jewel, lies that sleeping fairy
princess set high among the silent fells, whose
sleep song, 'mid indescribable silence—the silence
that can be felt and almost seen, is the soughing
of the larches and the deeper sound like the
rushing of waters, made by the fir trees whose
rich brown stems make the vistas through the
wood so lovely.

And out from this wood there juts out, right
into the little lochan or tarn, a very welcome and
noble headland crowned with those red-stemmed
Scotch firs which are mirrored in the dark water.
Yes, Grisedale Tarn is fine ; she lies higher,
under a greater mountain. She breathes the air

BLEA TARN AND LANGDALE PIKES.

of two thousand feet up which is much more rarefied, and she is indifferent of ornament. She dwells among the highest peaks too, under nobly named Helvellyn; but for beauty and richness, daintiness and grace she cannot compare with Blea Tarn.

CHAPTER XXXI

AFTER a good long look at the mountain princess
we turn and note the sides of Blaikrigg on the
western side of the glen, with its slopes of yellow
grass faded to that soft chamois-yellow, of which
I have spoken, and fringed with broad stretches
of bracken. From these rich, soft colours the
eye wanders to the patches of heather, long since
turned black on Blaikrigg's topmost stretches.
Finally we note above the lake the massive outline of the Langdale Pikes peering over the fells
on the north-eastern side like some monstrous
giants' heads, or the figure of Polyphemus which
towers above the galley of Ulysses in Turner's
great picture.

And here again silence is made acute by the
swishing of the larches, the murmuring of distant
streams and the cry of the carrion crow which

haunts these mountain regions in search of the carcases of the sheep that die or get crag-fast and exhausted on the fells.

And now we cross the grass again to the track at the entrance gate and get a new view to the westward, of the snow-sprinkled crags of Blaikrigg stretching along the opposite side of the valley. While behind it on the north we see the fine outline of the Pike o' Blisco which offers its front against the opposing mass of Langdale Pikes lying on the other side of the valley.

Blea Tarn Cottage

We have reached the famous Blea Tarn Cottage where dwelt the Solitary described in " The Excursion." It is the only house in the glen and appears to be practically unaltered since Wordsworth's time. Wordsworth and his companion had their meal in the room on the floor above. To-day the oak-beamed kitchen hung with great store of bacon is the tea - room. Wordsworth describes the scene :—

> . . . All at once, behold !
> Beneath our feet, a little lowly vale,
> A lowly vale, and yet uplifted high
> Among the mountains ; even as if the spot

> Had been from eldest time by wish of theirs
> So placed, to be shut out from all the world !
>
> . . . . . .
>
> With rocks encompassed . . .
>
> . . . . . .
>
> A liquid pool that glittered in the sun,
> And one bare dwelling ; one abode, no more !
> It seemed the home of poverty and toil,
> Though not of want : the little fields, made green
> By husbandry of many thrifty years,
> Paid cheerful tribute to the moorland house.
>
> . . . . . .
>
> Ah ! what a sweet recess, thought I, is here !
> Instantly throwing down my limbs at ease
> Upon a bed of heath ;—full many a spot
> Of hidden beauty have I chanced to espy
> Among the mountains, never one like this ;
> So lonesome and so perfectly secure.

In the cottage Wordsworth describes the dainties which overspread the board — " oaten bread, curd, cheese, and cream and cakes of butter curiously embossed."

> Butter that had imbibed from meadow-flowers
> A golden hue, delicate as their own
> Faintly reflected in a lingering stream.
>
> Nor lacked . . .
> Our table, small parade of garden fruits,
> And whortle-berries from the mountain side.

The tea Miss Weir, the present hostess at Blea Tarn Cottage, put before us was not less ample. Indeed it included a number of the very good cakes common amongst the excellent cooks of the Lake District and a " pound cake " worthy of Bond Street. No less hospitable than the hostess was the big sheep dog who had a snug bed by the great fire.

From the cottage the mountains to be seen on the left to the west are Blaikrigg, Great End, Bowfell, Shelter Crags and Pike o' Blisco. The Langdale Pikes are visible on the right and to the south-west lie Wetherlam and the Coniston group.

The journey back to Ambleside through Great Langdale is easy. After a long descent down the very loose Blea Tarn Road—a road quite impossible to cycles—there is one of the best and least hilly roads in the Lake District through Chapel Stile and Clappersgate to Ambleside.

CHAPTER XXXII

LAKELAND'S WILD ANIMALS

In the great forests which covered large part of Westmorland, Western Cumberland and the Furness district, Camden, whose mother was a Curwen of the Workington family, states that the buck, the doe, the wild boar were common up to the twelfth century and the wild boar till the end of the sixteenth century. Horns and antlers are still sometimes unearthed on the fells. The wolf is supposed to have disappeared some centuries earlier.

The fox is, of course, the most notable of the wild creatures remaining on the hills. He is a very clever and witty fellow so much so that I must confess to sympathising with him rather than with the men and the hounds that hunt him. The fox is also handsome, and a very plucky fighter against long odds. Indeed were it not that he has a great partiality for a diet consisting largely of poultry, there is no doubt that he would have become a very respectable member of society. Of course I know that other persons have a partiality for poultry—city aldermen notably, but that fact, while it proves the fox's good taste and discrimination, seals his doom. There cannot be two kings in Brentford, as the old proverb has it, nor can a rival for the good things of Leadenhall Market be tolerated at the Mansion House.

Many good stories are told in which the fox has been too much for the dog and also too much for the man. Indeed, the general opinion among fox - hunting men in the Lake District is that it is the combination of the man and the dog that is too much for him. Were it not for the human hunter it is probable that very many of the thirty-five foxes which have been killed this season (April 1921) would still be enjoying the best poultry both for supper and for breakfast.

Indeed one might go a little further and say that fleet and brave and intelligent as the Fell hound is, if he were no bigger than the fox and fought him alone over hill and dale instead of in packs, the fox would every time prove the better man of the two.

In short if he had been as tamable as the dog he would have attained high rank in the social scale.

One writer says that the superior condition of the hounds over that of the fox is the chief factor in enabling them to bring their quarry down.

This is, I think, quite wrong. Food for the body is very important, but food for the mind is more so in a race over the fells. The fox is better educated. He knows every nook and corner, every ledge, every crag, and he has learnt things the dogs don't know.

Then the fox of the fells can drop a distance of thirty to forty feet without serious injury and he can climb up steep rocks where no hound can follow. On rough ground he is thoroughly at home, and he can jump the highest fences though Mr. Richard Clapham points out he always does it sideways. I don't care how he does it; no doubt he being always on the defensive, has learnt things about hunting and being hunted that are not known even to my friend Mr. W. C. Skelton who has told us so much about it in his book

THE ABODE OF "THE SOLITARY," BLEA TARN.

on the Coniston Hunt which is now being published.

The Lakeland Fell Pony

" The Fell Pony " of the Lake District is not of native origin. The native breed has died out; it was described by Pringle who wrote in 1794. He says the Westmorland horses were small and not exceeding 14½ hands and though said to be hardy, were neither strong nor handsome.

The present Fell pony is a descendant of the Galloway of Southern Scotland, whose qualities, Pringle says, " were speed, stoutness and sure-footedness over very rugged and mountainous country." They were rather under 14 hands in height and were " essentially weight-carrying ponies," [1] very powerful and compact in build. The legs of the Fell pony of to-day have more bone than had the old native Westmorland breed, so says Mr. Wingate-Saul (1899) quoted in Mr. F. W. Garnett's excellent book on Westmorland Agriculture.

The Galloway rather than the Westmorland pony of the light type resembling those I have

[1] Youatt, 1831.

seen in the New Forest, must certainly have been
the beast used by the old moss-trooper. In
" Sweet Heather " a fine animal with a very small,
pretty and intelligent head and powerful neck
and shoulders we have, I suggest, the kind of
beast a Borderer would need to carry himself and
his plunder over long distances.

CHAPTER XXXIII

HUNTING ON LAKELAND HILLS

HUNTING in the Lake Country differs in very many respects from hunting in the Midlands and the South. In the Lake District the hunt lies over the hills many of which reach to 2000 feet some to 2600 feet or more.

From this it will be seen that the word " sport " in the Border counties means something quite different and distinct. It is much more primitive, depends less on artificial aids, and the horse which gallops in the Midlands after the fox over meadows and ploughed fields and jumps five-barred gates and waterways, is not in the picture. The grand scarlet hunting coat is only seen on the huntsman, and the charming young lady who constantly needed rescuing from sunk roads and quagmires and fallen steeds and who always married her rescuer, would never have entered into the novels of Charles Lever or Hawley Smart or Frank Smedley or Miss Braddon, if they had been bred in the heart of the hills of ancient Cumbria.

Clad in heavy hob-nailed boots and in ugly knickerbockers or graceful knee-breeches, and wearing not the picturesque braid bonnet or the glengarry of Scotland, nor yet the round hunting bonnet of the southern shires, but clad in that most hideous head-garment ever invented the " deer-stalker " or hooligan cap, the hunters follow the quarry.

And the road lies over wet mosses, through wet bracken, over black heather-clad boggy land, over rocks and precipices, through deep snow, across break-neck chasms, down which pour becks or burns only less dangerous than those you find in crossing the tops of the hills in Argyll or Inverness-shire. No place for petticoats certainly !

Then on the lower slopes you have to wade through deep woods of larch and birch and oak and short bracken and water—water everywhere; sometimes, also, there is impenetrable mist and rain and wind that put you in mind of the Arctic regions—if you have never been there.

For strong men it is the finest sport you could have—the finest sport for every one but the fox.

In Lakeland the hunt is thus on foot, and, needless to say is often very hard going. The fox too is followed right up to the tops of the hills amongst rocks and crags.   It is not uncommon for a dog in his excitement, to follow reynard on to some ledge of rock and to roll with him down to the stony places below and to return no more to his mates at the kennels of Patterdale, Ambleside, or wherever he comes from.

CHAPTER XXXIV

THE hound used for fox-hunting in Lakeland is a breed quite apart from the hound of the " Peterborough " type which is used in the Midlands. His height is 22½ inches at most, somewhat smaller than the southern type and he is altogether a tougher customer.

He will work on eight days a fortnight and will last up to his tenth season in full work. He will work over much harder, rougher ground on the fells and mountains. His whole life indeed, is a much harder one than that of his rival, and, important point, he is very fast, much more so than the southern hound.

Despite all these merits the hardy northerner fetches only the small sum of sixty shillings while, according to Mr. Clapham, the Warwickshire hound will fetch ninety pounds and the Radnor-shire twenty pounds.

There is one other interesting difference between these two types. The southern hounds have " cat " feet while the northern Fell hounds have " hare " feet.

I have found the Fell hound in private life as friendly as a beagle than which no dog is more loving. The puppies are delightful and as full of fun as kittens. The southern hound has a tendency to be sometimes serious and a little bit surly. The older dogs of both sorts are dignified. One day in an Ambleside by-path I saw a huge, bony, powerful old hound worrying a bone when out rushed a very fierce and quarrelsome grey-hound which lived on the spot and considered the approach to my den and his master's, as within his sphere of influence.

The greyhound, a splendid beast, bounded with a fierce growl at the old dog as though he would eat him. The old boy raised his head an inch or two, keeping his paw on the bone and for a moment eyed his rival, who catching one glint from the old dog's eye crouched back from his outstretched front paws and then slunk home across the green. Here was dignity and power and intelligence. A quarrelsome dog would have gone for the greyhound but the Fell hound is

not quarrelsome. It has also the merit of being
less fierce than his rival of Warwickshire, as, after
it has killed the fox, it will not touch the carcase,
whereas a Warwick or Radnor hound will tear it
to pieces. In other words, the Lakeland hound
is more of a gentleman in his cups.

WILD MOUNTAIN PONIES, ANGLE TARN, PATTERDALE.

CHAPTER XXXV

THE PRETTIEST LAKELAND SPORT

YET another Lake District sport and an interesting
one. It is not, however as distinctively Lakeland
as the Hound Trail, for in many sheep-farming
districts it is common. I refer to the Sheep-dog
Trials, more interesting to the spectator than
even the Hound Trail. How is it done? Three
sheep are taken out of a field for each competition.
The man takes his stand near the judge's box,
wearing a leash round one arm so that he cannot
advance towards his dog. From his stand he
directs the dog who has to drive the three sheep
between two flags through hurdles, and from the
hurdles to the pen. The master directs his dog
by whistling or waving his arms or by hallooing,
or by all three. At the pen he leaves his stand and
goes forward to help his dog to drive the sheep
into the pen through its narrow entrance. This is

a very difficult task. The man and dog who does these operations in the shortest time gets the prize.

Sheep-dog trials are held all over the Lake District; amongst them is the well-known Rydal Show held on August 23rd where I was present. The winner of the first prize, in the class open to all comers, was the five-year-old dog Nettie, who was cleverly engineered by her master, Mr. J. V. Allen, Deepdale. She made the round and penned in 5 min. 42 sec. She took the first prize of ten guineas and Lord Kerry's silver challenge cup.

Mr. J. J. Leak, Troutbeck Park, came next with his black and tan four-year-old Bob in 6 min. 5 sec. The finish was exciting, and was heartily cheered.

Mr. Mason, Kirkby Lonsdale, did brilliantly with his Floss, an eight-year-old, and came in third with her in 7 min. 34 sec. His second dog, Laddie, five years, a wonderfully clever animal, failed only at the pen, up to which his time was the record one of 1 min. 20 sec. through the flags and 3 min. 5 sec. to the hurdles. The failure was not on the dog's part; he made never a fault, being as wise as an owl but less noisy. He and his master were loudly applauded.

Mr. T. D. Handley, Ravenstonedale, was fourth with his clever bitch Nell, of only one and a half years. She was admirably engineered by her master, who took everything quietly, never, as they say in golf, " pressing " either his dog or his sheep. They went through like a piece of machinery. At the pen two sheep entered, but the third went off at a right angle, and stood by the entrance outside the pen. Mr. Handley then showed again his knowledge of sheep nature —which is very like human nature in this, that it follows the mob. He made no excited rush, did not wave his arms like a semaphore ; he quietly moved away from the entrance where the sheep stood hesitating, to the opposite side of the pen. The sheep, thus left, determined that it could not face the world alone—so few have pluck to do that—it walked quietly in among its pals ! The crowd cheered : they knew that this time the man had proved wiser even than his dog. The sheep almost enjoyed it ; they were never once frightened : whereas it must be admitted that in most cases they were a good deal chivvied about. All these momentous decisions of sheep and shepherd took only 7 min. 42 sec.

It is satisfactory to know that the sheep only once go through this performance; a new set of sheep must be taken each time under the rules.

CHAPTER XXXVI

WHAT is a Hound Trail? Few people outside the Lake District could answer that question. It is one of the sports peculiar to Wild Lakeland.

A drag or trail is laid on the hills by two men known as " trail layers " who must be very familiar with the district. The drag consists of a bag steeped in oil of aniseed which the men carry. One of the men starts from the most distant point which is to be reached by the hounds ; the other starts from the winning-post.

The drag is laid every quarter of a mile and is pressed to the earth with the foot.

The starter marshals the dogs, who are tremendously keen to get away ; indeed, one of the pleasant things about the hunt is to see their eagerness and to hear them. They disappear, leaping walls—the grey stane dykes or other obstacles in splendid style, and streaming through the bracken and the heather ; now out of sight, now flashing into the open on the hill-side a thousand feet up.

The crowd waits expectant in the meadow far below and, when the dogs get on to the homeward trail and flash one after another, far apart out into the open, the excitement is intense and the shrieks and whistling of the owners of the competing dogs make the welkin ring. The time for the round averages about twenty-five minutes.

The dogs are as full of excitement as their masters and thoroughly enjoy themselves. A Hound Trail is probably the most popular sport in Lakeland. No athletic meeting or agricultural society's show or football association sports, is considered complete without a Hound Trail. The prizes range from about £5 for the winner and £3 and £2 for the runners-up. A good dog can bring in a substantial sum to his owner in a season.

The hound used is lighter than the foxhound and faster. They are trained by their owners or by members of families noted as dog-trainers. The men " walk " them and the hounds live in their homes and, having this great advantage of family life, are remarkably clever and friendly.

The sport is governed by the Hound Trailing Association, a body which, I understand, sets its face against any kind of mutilation now including, I hope and believe, the absurd and cruel custom, which I have seen practised, of clipping the coats of the dogs with a horse clipper.

A dog with his coat clipped almost to his skin, must be a very unhappy and uncomfortable fellow as, indeed, he looks. I have seen dogs also that look very underfed, and no one will convince me that a dog whose backbone looks like a band-saw, is at his best or brightest any more than a very lean man is.

It is, I am sorry to say, the small private owner who has inherited these mistaken methods. A dog that looks miserable and unhappy should be disqualified; because no dog looks unhappy without a very sound reason for it.

It should be said that the dogs of the local and famous packs like the Coniston, ·of which Mr. Skelton has written, are models in the matter of condition. They are also the happiest and handsomest lot of fellows you could see anywhere.

CHAPTER XXXVII

FROM Grisedale Tarn the ascent up Dollywaggon Pike on to Helvellyn of which it forms part, can be made. It may not be the easiest way to reach Helvellyn but it is perhaps the most full of interest because, in the route we get the home of Frank Bramley, the fine ascent up the shoulder of Seat Sandal (if we take the left-hand footpath), and the fine views of Coniston Lake and of the sea at Morecambe. We also get a view of Fairfield which cannot be obtained from any other place and a new view of Stone Arthur. The " hause " or narrow pass through which we reach the Tarn is interesting, as, once through it, the world in which we have been sojourning—the Ambleside-Rydal-Grasmere world—is quite shut out and the Ullswater and eastern hills generally, come into view, with great Blencathara and others to the north. The name is seemingly made up of " blen " a tongue and " cathir " [1] a fort not seat or saddle as has been suggested, the tongue-shaped hill of the fort is another example of the splendid possibilities of the Keltic in names which are carefully descriptive and at the same time sonorous and musical.

Because Helvellyn has one or two precipitous and dangerous places it is generally assumed that it is a difficult hill to climb but this is quite a mistake. An experienced Alpine climber who went up Helvellyn seven or eight times says, it is " the easiest mountain to ascend from any point that is possible." He meant that there are, of course, certain points from which most mountains are impossible.

This great hill like many others, looks best in my opinion, from a distance. From Grisedale and Ullswater it impressed me most. The summit is bare and, like some other mountain summits, disappointing. The best view of a hill is not obtained by looking down upon it from a greater height, in my judgement, but in looking at it from a spot below from which we can get an uninterrupted view, a view over a valley for instance. Such a view we get of Bowfell, Crinkle

[1] *See page* 109.

LOW WATER TARN, CONISTON.

Crags, Scawfell, from the Windermere-Ambleside road ; from Lake Road Windermere, from Waterhead, Ambleside ; from Jenkin Crag and other points.   These views are finer than anything you can get from the summit of Helvellyn or of Wansfell or most other hills.

The really interesting thing about Helvellyn is the curious effect of the south-eastward moving glacier of some twenty-five thousand years since, when it broke on the rocky ridge and sharpened in its descent the razor-like Striding Edge.   As it plunged downward it left this grandly curved and noble precipice, which is the greatest beauty of the mountain.

It does not seem to have been noticed that a very similar precipice can be seen towards evening when the shadows are dark and velvety in looking up from Waterhead to High Pike the larger of the beautiful peaks that dominate the east side of the Rothay Valley overlooking the Scandale burn and glen.

To those who judge a mountain by its height rather than by its beauty or grandeur of outline; or who consider that a view in which you get glimpses of six counties is necessarily better than a view of Blencathara or Schiehallion or Ben Cruachan at

ten miles distance, Low Pike 1637 feet and High
Peak, his grand compatriot, will not appeal.

To me the view of them from the road near
Waterhead (I have seen them excellently from the
motor coach) with the glacier-made edge of High
Pike and its deep shadow below, is much better
worth seeing than Striding Edge the real beauty
of which can only be realised from a distance, as
when seen close at hand, we are too near to get
its great shadows.

Distance and high lights and deep shadows
and mist are one half of landscape, and colour
and cloud effects are the other half. The part-
draped beauty is the most subtle and attractive,
because suggestion inspires us while discovered
facts leave us unmoved.

Sometimes, however, a mountain may make
an appeal to us of another kind, kin to that made
by a noble outline—by its grand cliffs and its
black, jagged rocks — " for ever shattered and
the same for ever." There is much of that
appeal made by Striding Edge and by the grand
view of the angular ridges of Red Screes (seen
from the height above Caiston Glen) with their
red colour and the deep drop to Brothers Water
and the Kirkstone Pass far below.

The fine crags and precipices of Ill Bell, of Blaikrigg, and the Arabian Nights touch about those tremendous caves on Loughrigg Terrace, with their dripping roofs and great lakes full of green water; these are also among the haunting memories of Lakeland.

CHAPTER XXXVIII

From the Kirkstone Pass the road beyond Hartsop
towards Patterdale and Ullswater needs no more
climbing. By the Grasmere route, however, there
is a climb from Grisedale Tarn which can be done
even by an indifferent walker.

From Hartsop Bridge the road lies below
the great High Street Roman Causeway, one of
the most wonderful works of the wonderful people
who built that greatest of all our national monu-
ments—the most impressive and the most inspir-
ing—the great Roman wall.

On the right we pass the road to closely hidden
Hayes Water and the burn that leads up into
Caudle Moor. Above is Mardale and the grand
Ill Bell, 2478 feet above sea-level, and Thorn-
thwaite Crag below which the Roman road passes,
intersected by many ancient paths and pony

tracks.   Below Ill Bell is the Kentmere reservoir, the mere at Kentmere itself having long since been drained as nearly dry as you can drain anything in that region.   The river Kent rises between Harter Fell and Lingmell, close to the famous Nan Bield Pass.   To the south is Garburn Pass above, the deep, and splendid valley of the Kent which gives its name to the town of Kendal.

This hill region is very different in character from the hills to the westward ; save for the picturesque group of hills which overshadow the Kirkstone Pass—Ill Bell, Great Dodd, John Bell's Banner and Dove Crag it is a region of round, flat-topped summits which become a little bleak and monotonous, resembling in this the fells of Shap and the cold, wind-swept heights of the Pennine Chain, which rise grandly out of the flat rich valley of the Eden.

Patterdale and Glenridding

Some two miles beyond Hartsop, if we keep to the main road, we have, on the hills above, Angle Tarn and the great stretch of Martindale Forest.   On the other hand we have a road that leads to the fine valley of Deepdale.   We are now

in Patterdale which is watered by the Gold Rill,
beck or burn—all these words mean the same.
The names Patrickdale and St. Patrick's Well may
date from early Christian times or from the eleventh
century when Gospatrick, cousin of the Scottish
king, Malcolm Canmore, was Earl of Northumberland and owner of a great part of present Cumberland and Westmorland. The first part of his
name " Guas " was the British equivalent to
Gaelic *gille* a follower and he represented, of
course, the Gaelic Kelt, but was also a great-great-
grandson of Ethelred II. of England. He was
therefore seventh in descent from King Alfred
and was the chief representative of the kin of
St. Columba, who were kings of those Scots who
first brought Christianity and a higher civilisation
to their kinsmen in tongue and in blood, the
northern and southern Picts as Ninian had done
to the Picts of Galloway nearly a century earlier.

Thomas Hardy, the great novel-writer of our
day, tells us the story of " Tess " who sprang
from imaginary D'Urbervilles, but her romance
cannot compare in historic interest with the fact
that in Lakeland and in other parts are still
representatives of Gospatrick and his forebears.

CHAPTER XXXIX

ULLSWATER AND HELVELLYN

NOT only the families but the older place-names tell of the Gael and not the Briton as words like Glenriddan and Glencoin, Dove (Dubh that is black) Crag and Aird Beck suggest.

Patterdale and Glenridding stand at the head of Ullswater, which is one of the grandest of the English lakes and in length second only to Windermere.

On the whole the scenery in this district is wilder, barer, bleaker, than it is further to the west. The colouring is less brilliant. Round Stybarrow the woods are, however, very fine and the walk to the waterfall at Aira Force is perhaps the best thing to be seen at Ullswater Head. The walk along the lake towards Penrith too, is magnificent.

Nearly all the names round here are of English

origin or, more correctly perhaps, of Teutonic origin, and they certainly do not carry with them any touch of romance, " Watson's Dodd," " Stybarrow Dodd," " Sticks Pass " for instance. Here and there, however, we get the grand music of the older names, left by the Kelts before they learnt English from the prosaic husbandmen who settled amongst them. For instance Helvellyn, Blencowe, Penruddock, Penrith, Glenderaterra while Mungrisdale to the north reminds us of a Keltic missionary who brought Christianity to the heathen English—St. Kentigern, otherwise St. Mungo, the friend of Columba.

That was in the sixth century, thirteen hundred years ago.

At Glenridding are the Greenside lead mines which are now lying idle. The mining village up the Glen is a rather rambling and untidy place. In 1847 one hundred men were employed in these mines.

From Patterdale and Glenridding there are tracks which lead to Helvellyn, and Swirrel Edge and Wythburn, and to Place Fell and St. Sunday Crag, among the grandest bits of mountain scenery in the Lake District—also to Dollywaggon and Grisedale Tarn and Grasmere. No one should try any of these hills for the first time without the guidance of some one who knows the neighbourhood, nor should he go unprovided with food.

From the head of Ullswater there is a fine walk by Dunmallet and the splendid green pastures of Dalemain and the clear stream of Eamont (" Yamont ") to quaint, stony, cosy Penrith. As we near the town we pass the historic and beautiful old tower of the Threlkelds—Yanwith Hall. It is a fine specimen of the better-class Border fortress.

Hereabouts, sometimes in the castle itself, Sir Lancelot Threlkeld sheltered his stepson the Shepherd Lord, " Clifford of Cumberland " from the time of the terrible battle of Towton where Clifford's father was killed, as described by Shakespeare. It was not till the accession of Henry VII. that the young lord was restored to his dominions which included the great castle of Brougham near Penrith, Brough Castle south of Appleby, and Skipton in Yorkshire.

Near to the head of Ullswater is a house called Eusmere which was built by a famous man—famous in the best sense,—a man who fought a hard and gallant fight against vested interest.

This was Thomas Clarkson who did more than any man to do away with that shameful slavery which allowed human beings to be actually bought and sold. Slavery is still with us but not in this crude form. To-day a man may move about from town to town from county to county and may change his employer. The African slave could do none of these things before the days of Clarkson and his thirty years' fight against those who had made fortunes, as was said, " by the black blood of the African."

CHAPTER XL

THE KINGS OF PATTERDALE

In Patterdale a family long flourished at Goldrill Cottage and later at Patterdale Hall, who bore the title of " Kings of Patterdale." Some of the name (Mounsey) still remain in the district I think. It appears that in the days of the Border raids a party of Scots moss-troopers rode down into this valley as they had the habit of doing, sometimes penetrating into Lancashire, Durham and Yorkshire. On this particular occasion the shepherds of the Ullswater fells were summoned by Mounsey, one of their number, so the story goes. He proved to be a very Napoleon, a prodigy of valour and of strategy, for he actually defeated the Scots. This it would seem had never before been accomplished, for they decided to make him king of their district. The family held the title for many generations and were the leaders in all things great and small.

So onerous indeed were the duties imposed on the members of the family which had put forth a man who could defeat the Scots, that at last one of them asked leave to abdicate, and so the kingdom of Patterdale reverted to the British Crown. We are not all born to stand before the footlights !

From this it must not be assumed that the people of the Border were all enemies. The organised clans right up on the Border were not enemies but quite the opposite. In a raid by the Scots in 1587 Sir Cuthbert Collingwood after a defeat, was able to bring up more men and, following, " overtook some of the Scots footmen and five or six were slain and some 150 taken prisoners, for these countrymen," Carey who tells the story writes, " will not willingly kill any of them " (the Scots).

This particular raid was made by the men of Liddesdale, Eusdale, Annandale and Teviotdale and was led by Buccleugh and Cessford—skilful and daring soldiers.

Edward Aglionby said a little later that the " Governance of Scotland (on the Border) most offensive to England was largely in two wards—in Annandale and Liddesdale."

Again he says " Lyddisdale is the most offensive countrie against both the West and the Middle Marches . . . the strength of the country consists of two surnames of Armestranges and Elwoodes." [1]

[1] That is Elwands, corrupted later into Elliots.

CHAPTER XLI

RAVENGLASS AND BLACK COMBE

THE SEA'S HARVEST ON THE CUMBRIAN COAST

Oh, the sea's grim steeds are snowy white,
   But red is the toll they ride to take,
   And red is the sorrow in their wake
In the dark and stormy night.

To-day the sea's wild horses whine and hiss,
   And full are they of fierce intent,
   Though two days gone like lambs they went,
When mothers and wives took their last kiss.

One line of thin grey foam they were all week,
   Listless as though there none were left to ride
   Upon their backs and dash aught else aside ;
And all the level sands lay brown and sleek.

To-night the wild horses rise in war array
   Some five lines deep, and, as each poised rank breaks,
   Behind their backs they fling the fierce white flakes,
Flushing the beach with showers of glittering spray.

Strange they should strive so ; that they seek to rend
  The ships that by the silver shores are strown,
  While widows lift their hands and weep and moan ;
Ah ! who shall tell the wherefore—to what end ?

'Tis said He walks the sea and yes, He knows,
  His hand can place the bit that gives them pause,
  Within those ivory, white, foam-flecked jaws ;
Thus sadly then He reaps and yet—He sows !

Oh, the sea's grim steeds are snowy white,
  But red is the toll they ride to take,
  And red is the sorrow in their wake
In the dark and howling night.
                              MacKenzie MacBride.

BLACK COMBE stands like a sentinel on the stormy
coast of Cumberland.   In the opinion of Wordsworth the view from the flat tableland at its top
is the finest in the Lake District.   It is certainly
the most extensive view in Lakeland but according to Colonel Mudge of the Ordnance Survey,
the hill commands the widest view in Great
Britain.   From it fourteen English and Scottish
counties can be seen—if you are anxious to see
them all at once—and westward Ireland ; southward the grim bare Yorkshire hills.   Near home
we have Seathwaite and Broughton in Furness
and the Valley of the Duddon ; the Isle of Walney
and Piel Castle ; also Lancaster Castle ; the

Welsh mountains, the Irish Sea, the Isle of Man ;
the Cumberland coast from Whitehaven to the
swift - ebbing sands of Solway. Beyond, Criffel
and Cairnsmore and the other great hills of
Galloway stand like a rampart.

RAVENGLASS—A PRE-ROMAN SEAPORT TOWN

There are two roads by which Black Combe
can be reached with a walk of not more than six
miles. One is from the little town of Bootle on
the Furness Railway, the other is from Broughton
station. It can also be reached from the seaport
of Ravenglass.

Though now much decayed, and even a little
bit squalid Ravenglass is a place of great historic
interest. It was a port in Roman times and
certainly before those times, judging by its
ancient name. With it a network of roads was
connected.

There all the wares of the Continent were
landed, and the produce of the country was put
upon foreign vessels.

Ravenglass is an excellent starting - place for
rambles, the walk to Black Combe is only seven
miles and the same number of miles will take

STRIDING EDGE, HELVELLYN.

you to Boot, at the foot of Scawfell, either by walking or by the little railway from Ravenglass.

From the antiquarian point of view nearly all the interesting spots in a district which is not rich in antiquities or romantic memories (apart from its scenery) lie scattered around the town, so that it is to my thinking, the best of all centres on the eastern side.

From it the historic castle of Muncaster is only a mile and a half distant. It is grandly placed above the Esk, which flows past the town. Very historic is also, Egremont Castle; it belonged to the de Multon family who took the name of the heiress of the Lucys, whom one of them married. The castle was built by the great Earl of Chester, William le Meschen. Five miles from Egremont is Calder Abbey, a charming spot. This was also founded by Ranulf, Earl of Chester, a member of the same family, in 1134.

Near Black Combe again, there is a monument of great antiquity. It is what people, for want of a better name, call a druidical temple. It stands at Swinside, right among the hills and measures no less than 285 feet round. Within this circle are fifty-four upright stones.

It has been pointed out that in the neighbourhood of ancient remains of this kind, the rowan
tree (mountain ash) generally grows plentifully.
The superstition is that the witches or evil spirits
would not come near this tree. In the West
Highlands the ash tree is to be found, at all the
older farm-house doors. If, in wandering about
the hills, I see a solitary ash tree I expect to find
the ruins of a farm-house beside it. The superstition is that the ash was the wood of which the
Cross was made.

The rowan was especially popular because of
its red berries, so was the fuchsia tree, which
we see in every West Highland graveyard. Its
berries are still called " sacred drops."

The Temple can easily be included in a visit
to Black Combe, especially if a start is made from
the station of the Furness railway at Ravenglass.

CHAPTER XLII

GARBURN PASS FROM TROUTBECK

Its Great Surprise

THERE are few lonelier tracks than that ancient pack - horse road which leads from Troutbeck up to Garburn Pass. There is an approach to it also by Orrest Head which joins the track later.

From the lower road we have to go over the first stone bridge after passing Troutbeck church. There is a short climb to the farm-house. From the dip in the hill made by the stream we get a good view of the finely shaped cone of Ill Bell and the group of hills which rise above the Kirkstone Pass. What complaint Ill Bell suffers from I know not, but whatever it is it must be a chronic complaint. But then Ill Bell may be a mere vulgar dropping of the letter " h " and his name may be Hill Bell all the time.

Ill or well, Bell has a noble front and I don't know what the Troutbeck valley would do without him.

Close by on the hill called High Street are the remains of a Roman road.

Nothing in their history, as some writer has said, impresses one with the greatness of the Romans so much as the sight of the remains of the Roman wall on the Northumberland and Cumberland border. The roads which passed, like the Maiden way over Cross Fell in the Pennines; or in Westmorland and Cumberland over the tops of remote hills, are almost as wonderful. Nothing stopped the Roman; on he went methodically, solidly.

From the bridge we can see a long stretch of the glittering stream fringed with trees and above it these noble hills.

At the farm we turn to the left and pass through a gate on to the old pack-horse track, or climb the hill to get a short cut. Short cuts are, in my experience, and I have been lost and had to sleep out on the hills, very long cuts, and it is much better to keep to the road or track.

It is true that in many parts the road is more like a waterfall than a road, but the short cut is probably worse! It is a steady climb, and the surface of the track is awful, but we are repaid by the keen air and the blusterous wind, fresh as a breeze from Lapland.

The Tongue

On our right we have a high bank and on our left the prettiest view of the Troutbeck Valley, as we can here see the Tongue which fills the top end. And all the time we are approaching Applethwaite Common which is on our left. It fills up all the southern corner of the valley and as we approach becomes more varied and lovely in colour. First we have only the bracken and dead grasses which give a fine contrast to the browns and reds. And now a stray shaft of sunlight rests upon the bronze and wine-red brae. The track lies through a farmyard—a sheep-dog puts his head out of a window upstairs, a kitten skips daintily over the wet path ; a very fine fat boy with very rosy cheeks opens the gate, and we are out on the track. We have on our left the red brae with its two lovely patches of apple-green making the reds so brilliant. From here we get an excellent view of Wansfell, filling all the opposite side of the glen.

The track now faces east and we have fine new views of Ill Bell and High Street and of a deep corrie on the nearer hill above. In the head of Troutbeck Glen we have some splendid velvet shadows and, looking back, can see Windermere in a blaze of light. Our road lies between old stone dykes and high over one of these a picturesque group of sheep gaze down upon my friend and myself. All this beneath a very blue sky, and blue skies are not common here among the mountains.

Personally I prefer the mountains under a grey and cloudy sky. Then it is we get the most wonderful and mysterious effects. However, when the frost is " nipping rarely " and the wind is whistling round the crags and rushing through the deep corries, then a blue sky fits well the sense of exhilaration one has among the mountain-tops.

But to-day the blue sky is not everywhere, for, looking back from this height we can see the distant hills to the westward—Black Combe and Scawfell, very dim and grand.

Grassy Troutbeck lies now far below us, and we are still rising. The red braes to our left become even finer as we go up the long slope. The deep corrie above has a blue velvet shadow with a margin of bright sage-green with mottled shadows. To the right we have the bright red brae. We agree, my friend and I, that the head of the valley is the finest part of it.

The place is here absolutely bare of trees or of the homes of men ; to the north-east we have still Ill Bell and his neighbours, and on the nearer hill-sides there is now an unexpected depth of colour—red, yellows ; soft greens, very light in tone, and, behind the luminous fell slopes—the same blue patch of shadow beyond.

Northwards we can see Red Screes now very well, and all the Kirkstone region and, at this closer range, the contour of Ill Bell comes out very clearly as does the nearer hillside with its bottle-green grass and bleached velvety patches of sage green. Below we see the point where the Troutbeck road crosses into the Kirkstone road.

As we approach the Pass we can, looking backward, get another glimpse of Scawfell and Great Gable and, to the north-east, of the snowy peak of Helvellyn, as also of Bowfell and all the Windermere giants.

At the summit the scene is made sombre by

the deep brown almost black, of the faded heather
on the northern slopes above the Pass.

Looking over the succession of sloping ridges
backed by the deep blue shadow of Red Screes,
the scene is very fine, very wild.

Head of the Pass

We have now reached the summit, and we turn
our backs towards Troutbeck valley and enter
the long hidden, Garburn Pass. It is short.
I lingered for a moment and my friend went
forward. I then followed my friend and as I rose
saw him below me. He was gazing over at a most
impressive sight—a deep valley had suddenly
yawned below us full of rocky shapes. To the
east were a succession of hills forming part of the
Pennine Chain, and right opposite high up in
the mist dim " in ancient fastnesses of twilight,"
were the monsters of the Yorkshire hills, the
western spur of the Pennines, touched here and
there with yellow half light like giants in some
mysterious giant land.

It is a surprise view of which I have not seen
the equal in all I know of Lakeland.

It was strange that the most neglected of

A SUDDEN SHOWER, BLEA TARN

Lake District climbs should have yielded so much pleasure ; for not one of the tourist books does more than mention Garburn Pass. What I was told by the natives was merely that the Pass itself was pretty, whereas though the Pass has fine views, in itself it is not pretty and there is very little of it. The view from it is mysterious and wonderful.

CHAPTER XLIII

THOMAS HOGARTH THE SATIRIST

TROUTBECK, like Ambleside, stands at one of two openings in those hills, which, since Roman times, were regarded as a natural rampart between the south and the Scottish and Pictish hosts who made the fat valleys of Westmorland their hunting ground. Next to the Kirkstone Pass and Ambleside Valley, the Troutbeck valley which forks off at the Kirkstone inn was the road most frequented by cattle lifters.

All the roads into Troutbeck are hilly, but the road up from Low Wood by the footpath and through the planting and over the Holbeck by the bridge, is the prettiest.

The easiest way is, however, the road from Troutbeck Bridge which leads you close by the river, to Town End.

Besides its claims to notice for beauty and the picturesqueness of its old houses, its farm buildings and spinning galleries, the Troutbeck dwellers in the past possessed individuality and character. They were prominent in their day for their appreciation of art, for one of them was a satirist and playwright who, in and about the year 1700, wrote plays which drew great audiences. This was Thomas Hoggart or Hogarth, originally Hogherd.

I have shown elsewhere that the old idea that the Hogarth family, of which William Hogarth the painter came, sprang from Troutbeck was a mistake. Mr. Sessions, in his *Literary Celebrities of the Lake District*, spoke of Troutbeck as the ancestral home of the Hogarths. The writer of *Black's Guide*, 1879 edition, again states that Hogarth's father was born in the Troutbeck valley. This is repeated in the edition of 1919 of that excellent book. Atkinson, writing in 1850, gives Thomas as the brother of Richard and uncle of William, the painter, and states that " auld " Thomas was born about 1670.

This is impossible in view of the epitaph given by Adam Walker and written by Thomas Hogarth himself on the death of his daughter Anne in 1705.

She was then aged 38, so would be born in 1667, three years before the date (1670) given by Atkinson as that of her father's birth.

Some time ago in Ambleside I went into the cycle department of Mr. George Tyson's garage, and noticed an old carved panel standing on a window sill. On coming out I walked across to see it and found, on the left half, the letter " T " and below it " A " while on the opposite panel was the single letter " H " and beneath was the date 1693. I asked Mr. Tyson whether he knew whose initials they were ; he replied that the " H " represented the name of Hogarth and the other two letters were the initials of the husband and wife of one of the Hogarths of Troutbeck, but he had not been able to find out more than that.

Walker, who took part in one of Hogarth's plays stated I find, that " auld Hogart " left a son Thomas and a daughter. This Thomas Hogart married Agnes Birket—a famous Troutbeck surname. Thomas and Agnes were, I think, the pair whose initials figure on the panel of 1693. This Thomas, an anonymous writer stated thirty years ago, had no surviving children, and left his goods to one Woodburn, who married his sister.

The old cottage of Hogarth stood upon the site now occupied by the new District Bank —a commanding position, but a new house was built upon the spot after " auld Thomas Hogarth's " death, by one Wilson who appears to have bought the property from Woodburn. Amongst the old furniture and relics saved by Wilson from the old house, an anonymous Troutbeck correspondent now tells me, was the carved oak panel of the old Court cupboard. This went to one of the Brownes of Town End, Troutbeck, of an old Statesman's family, one of whom married Wilson's sister. This explains how it came to be sold at The Boot.

Hogarth, the painter, was born in Bartholomew Close, London, as is proved by the Parish Register. His father, who, it is most interesting to know, had literary leanings, was the son of a Bampton yeoman of Kirkbythore origin.

The painter's father, Richard Hogarth, had an uncle, this was Thomas " Hogart," or " Hoggherd," who really did settle at Troutbeck. He was certainly, Troutbeck's most remarkable man and ought not to be forgotten.

The late Sir Douglas Galton, that most penetrating thinker, whom I have often met at

the meetings of a certain public body, wrote a
book on the heredity or persistence of genius in
families. It is very interesting to find that Thomas
Hogarth of Troutbeck, William Hogarth's great-
uncle, was a pungent and vigorous writer of plays
and of verse and a biting satirist of local follies.

Certainly Hogarth's writings show a remarkable mental likeness to his grand-nephew the
painter. Take, for instance, his description of
the Parish Clerk of Windermere (which included
Troutbeck) in days when it must have needed so
much courage to criticise local men and manners
in that remote, inaccessible valley.

Astonishing success attended Hogarth's efforts.

Education at that time was much more wide-
spread and more literary than it became a century
later. The decline was due to the rise of the
manufacturing industries, the adoption of the
factory system and the buying up of the old
Lakeland " Statesmen " by the big landowners.

Old Hogarth's boldness and virility, at any
rate, must have been widely known, and it says
much for the people that the whole countryside
was interested in his plays.

One of these was, Walker says, " enacted on
St. James's Day, 1693, upon a scaffold at the

Moss Gap, Troutbeck." In another, " The Destruction of Troy," Walker himself took part. The whole story was represented—" the wooden horse, Hector dragged by the heels, the fury of Diomed, the flight of Æneas, and the burning of the city." The stage, he says, " was a fabrication of boards placed about six feet high, on strong poles; the greenroom was partitioned off with the same materials ; its ceiling was the azure canopy of heaven . . . there were more spectators for three days together than the three theatres in London would hold; and let me add," he says, " you never saw an audience half so well pleased."

Of Hoggart in his lighter vein the following verses, already referred to, are a specimen. They give an amusing glimpse of the Windermere of his day :—

UPON THE PRESENT CLERK OF WINDERMERE

Under these monumental stones
  A Parish Clerk doth lye,
A hogshead doth enclose his bones,
  For he was always dry.

His lips unto the tap are lay'd,
  His back to the bung-hole brink ;
Who knows although that he be dead,
  But he may dream of drink !

> To spare the fare of Charon's boat,
>   When he to Styx shall come,
> This barrel may save him a groat
>   To drink in Elysium.

The clerk later paid the penalty and, despite the warning given, does not appear to have joined the Blue Ribbon Army, if we may judge from the epitaph Hoggart wrote :—

On ye Late Clerk of Windermere

> Here lies interred the body of Harry Fisher,
> Who to the ale wife still was a well-wisher ;
> Resorting to the tap-house each holiday i' the morn,
> And where he found good ale he'd draw to th' afternoon ;
> While if he found the liquor to be stronger,
> Then did he draw the hours a quarter longer,
> Fy, Lachesis ! What hate was in thy breast,
> His clerkship's thread so early to untwist.
> Sure death is partial, Atropos a clown.
> That for one priest two clerks thus be cut down.

LINGMOOR TARN AND LANGDALE PIKES.

CHAPTER XLIV

" THE MORTAL MAN " is one of the most famous hostelries in all Lakeland and equally famous is its lost sign. Gainsborough's stolen " Duchess of Devonshire " has not been more talked about. In the sale I referred to at " The Boot " Troutbeck, at which the wall cupboard was bought by Mr. George Tyson, there were a number of paintings by Ibbetson who painted the sign. These pictures should be noted by Lake Country collectors, for Ibbetson was one of the most skilful of painters of Lakeland scenery.

At the sale there were offered an engraved portrait of Ibbetson himself, by R. Cooper, engraved by J. R. Smith (lot 160) : Brathay Bridge (157), Tam o' Shanter (159), Classical Landscape, 40 × 29 (152), Lodore (153), Woodland River Scene, pair (154 and 155), Old Bridge

House, Ambleside (156, water-colour). All the landscapes were by Ibbetson.

Ibbetson, whose name was Julius Cæsar, lived at or near Ambleside and married a daughter of a Windermere man, William Thompson. He was himself born at Scarborough (1759). Apprenticed to a ship painter at Hull, he showing talent, went to London and got a good knowledge of the work of the Dutch painters. He married at twenty years of age and his first Academy picture " A View of Northfleet " was exhibited in 1785. He spent some time in China and worked hard, but on his return home was unable to sell his pictures and amongst many other misfortunes he suffered the loss of eight of his children and in 1794 his wife died. In addition he found his servants had robbed him. After an attack of brain fever which followed these disasters he seems to have lost his will-power and gave way to drink, George Morland the painter, being the companion of his drinking-bouts. He was finally obliged to leave London to escape his creditors. He went to Liverpool and thence to Ambleside where with increased work, he was able to pay his debts.

At Troutbeck he painted the famous sign of

"The Mortal Man." He was later, invited to settle at Masham by Mr. Danby of Swinton Park, and there he died in 1817. His last work was reminiscent of his home in the Lake District. It was a view of Ambleside Market Place with the old buildings as they stood in 1801.

Though his name is so well known in Ambleside district, as far as I have heard no work of his can be seen there. At the sale at "The Boot," as will be seen, there were several of his works. It would be interesting to see them along with those of William Green, restored to Ambleside. Sir Lionel Cust said that as a painter of cattle and pigs Ibbetson has hardly been excelled in England. He added that his pictures of animals were much prized, especially in Yorkshire ; and that in his landscape painting he somewhat resembled Richard Wilson, R.A.

Ibbetson published *A Picturesque Guide to Bath*, *A Process of Tinted Drawing* and *An Accidence or Gamut of Painters in Oil and Water Colours*.

There was also in the sale at " The Boot " an oil-painting on a panel by " J. Martin," which was formerly the signboard of " The Traveller's Rest," Kirkstone Pass. There can be no doubt that this was the famous John Martin (a Northumbrian), whose name has also been linked with Lakeland.

According to local tradition his famous picture " The Plains of Heaven " was painted from the scene in Glen Scandale looking down over the hill-slopes towards Windermere and Furness, a very imposing spectacle. This was amongst the last pictures painted by Martin who, by the way, was then living at famous Lindesay House, Chelsea. His pictures, especially his impressive " Belshazzar's Feast " were greatly prized until towards the end of his career. Martin probably well knew the north of England. He was a native of Haydon Bridge near Hexham and no doubt the vast, rolling, rather dreary and colourless mountain slopes and broad valleys of the Pennines inspired him, suiting well the grim subjects he loved to depict.

CHAPTER XLV

TROUTBECK AND JENKIN CRAG

SIR WILLIAM WATSON AND SKELGILL

TROUTBECK in the next generation at least—for we are slow in giving to living genius the honour that is its due—will count among its memories the fact that our finest poet since Swinburne's day lived at Skelgill near Troutbeck. I refer to Sir William Watson who put into the following splendid verses the real case for Wordsworth :—

> Not Milton's keen translunar music thine,
> Not Shakespear's cloudless, boundless human view,
> Not Shelley's flush of rose on peaks divine,
> Nor yet the wizard twilight Coleridge knew.
>
> What hadst thou that could make so large amends
> For all thou hadst not, and thy peers possessed,
> Motion and fire, swift means to radiant ends ?
> Thou hadst for weary feet the gift of rest.

197

From Shelley's dazzling glow or thunderous haze,
From Byron's tempest anger, tempest mirth,
Men turned to thee and found—not blast and blaze,
Tumult of tottering heavens, but peace on earth.

Not peace that grows by Lethe, scentless flower,
There in white languors to decline and cease,
But peace whose names are also rapture, power,
Clear sight and love : for these are parts of peace.

Besides the old-world air, Troutbeck has some virtues of to-day—it is always easy to get a good meal there at most reasonable cost, and it has a handsome Institute where you can take shelter and read the papers for half an hour. The village has many memories of its strong men,— " Troutbeck Giants," its famous wrestlers, like Longmire, and of its humorous characters like bold Thomas Hoggarth.

Amongst its celebrities at one time was a retired Admiral of the Fleet. Nothing in Troutbeck went on without him, but on one Sunday morning the Admiral was late for church and, after a general pause, the parson commenced the service with the words, " We will now praise the Lord—— " when the Clerk bobbed up exclaiming " He's not coom yet, sir ! "

The return journey from Troutbeck to Ambleside can be made by a quite different route from that described in another chapter. On the journey to Troutbeck from Ambleside the traveller has his back to the great hills, but if on the return journey he takes the ancient Roman Road which, leaving Troutbeck a little west of the Post Office, follows along the side of Wansfell, he has the hills before him all the way. At the summit he comes to a gate on which the words " To Ambleside " are painted. From this point the road descends to Low Skelgill; it there crosses the Holbeck by a bridge and continues through the farm-yard of High Skelgill and Jenkin Crag, from which fine views may be seen, to the old Ambleside road, past Fisherbeck.

The reason why this road should be chosen for the return journey is that all the way from the gate marked " Ambleside " the traveller will as I have said have before him the giant hills lying at the head of Windermere on the western side —the grand battlements of Crinkle Crags like a Giant's fortress ; Bowfell and the monstrous, ever-changing shapes of the Langdale Pikes. If the peaks of the Scawfell group are difficult of approach and difficult to see from the country around, the Langdale Pikes are almost everywhere present. From this Troutbeck-Skelgill track the

scene is especially grand. Of course the view is
more extensive from the top, say of Wansfell,
but from the lower level we get a much fuller
sense of the height and grandeur of the hills.
They, as it were, thus retain some of their secrets,
their grace of outline, their glamour.

TROUTBECK FROM COOK'S HOUSE

Yet another route to Troutbeck, which was
originally in St. Martin's Parish, Bowness, as was
the present village of Windermere (Berthwaite)
and all Ambleside above the Stock river. That
is on the south side of it. The connection of
Troutbeck with Windermere has always been
close and the old road between them goes from
Cook's House and Miller Brow past Ragrigg to
the village of Bowness. So that after visiting
Troutbeck you can cross the valley at Town End
footbridge and find an excellent road leading to
the Windermere - Ambleside road below Orrest
Head.

LITTLE LANGDALE TARN.

CHAPTER XLVI

Peat-Cutting

Among the industries of Lakeland one of the oldest is peat cutting and drying. The district of Furness lying on both sides of Coniston Lake, was once covered with vast forests. The forest of Blawith lay on the west and evidences of its having been well wooded have been found in the form of trees—oak and fir—which have been dug up out of the mosses or peat-bogs, and these, Camden says, generally lay with their tops towards the east, the high winds being always from the west.

The fir tree has been planted extensively by suggestion of the Forestry Department on Belle Isle in Windermere and at Rydal during the last few years. The experiment has been very successful, because, no doubt, the conifer was once common to all this mountain region as to Scotland. It is in fact, the hardiest tree in Europe. It grows in the Alps on hills of 9000 feet. It is of course an evergreen and its small narrow leaf offers the least possible foothold for the snow. The rustling of its leaves when shaken by the wind is one of the great sounds of Nature, it is like the rush of a mighty cataract.

How did these vast forests of the Lake District disappear? Wood and peat were for centuries the only fuel; the peat has been extensively cut and the ground cleared. Little peat has been cultivated for its own sake since the introduction of coal, and the sphagnum and other roots from which it is formed in the wet fells have been rooted out. This accounts for the peat mosses being now much less extensive.

The woods have gone not by storms but probably because every landowner sold his timber whenever he was hard up—and that was often. He was generally too improvident or too poor to replant, or was in the hands of the Abbots and Priors of religious houses who were extensive lenders of money to distressed gentry.

Trees have been found in many of the peat

bogs far up on the hills so that there were at one time forests of which we know nothing.

Mr. F. J. Lewis gives the following as the composition of the three kinds of peat in the Cross Fell district. Recent peat—*Eriophorum, Sphagnum Callima.* Forest bed peat—*Betula alba, Alnus glutinosa, Lychrus diurna,* etc. Arctic bed peat—*Salix reticulata, S. Arbuscula, Arctostaphylos alpina.*

The plants of the forest bed peat, he says, suggest temperate conditions replacing the arctic conditions of the lowest deposits.

The alpine plants still grow in the Lake District.

The floating islands on Coniston Lake and Derwentwater are said to be formed of peat grown in shallow lakes or parts of lakes from aquatic plants.

One of the chief of the peat mosses is at Seathwaite near Coniston, which had previously been part of the vast forest of Furness. There the peat is often as much as forty feet thick. Similar mosses are also formed in the mountain tarns which have gradually filled up in this way. Two tarns, one almost completely filled up with peat, may be seen on the lower slope of Scandale, below Low Pike, just above and a little to the west of High Sweden Bridge. This moss ʼhas been formed during the past thirty years. In other parts—the Winster Valley for instance and at Brigsteer, the peat has, on the contrary, been undergoing a process of disintegration and decay.

In the Highlands I know lochs formed out of this decay of the peat caused by the lapping of water. These lakes have to my mind an uncanny look so that, though in much rambling amongst West Highland hills I seldom missed the chance of a swim, I never ventured into a peat loch.

The most beautiful and romantic of them in my remembrance is Loch Ossian which has with its white coral-like margin and rich red and green mosses, all the glamour and the suggestion of eld implied in its name. It lies high up on Rannoch Moor below Corrour on the road from Fort-William, south-east, into Perthshire and Bridge of Gaur. I once saw some very uncanny peat lochs in County Mayo on the wild, dreary, desolate peat-bog—the biggest in Ireland which occupies great part of that county. In these bogs the natives used to find the bog oak of which ornaments are made.   The trees lay far down in the morass.

In Westmorland and Cumberland as in the Highlands and in Ireland, the peat fires were kept burning in the houses from generation to generation and in some districts were re-kindled only once a year—on St. Bride's Day—February 1st. This is probably of very ancient origin as the saint was merely a survival of the old Keltic goddess of the hearth and home.   After her the kingdom of Brigantia, which included the Lake District, is believed to have been named.

CHAPTER XLVII

CHARCOAL-BURNING

BEFORE coal was discovered and used to any extent, all up and down the country there were small " bloomaries " or forges for the making of iron implements, swords and other articles.

In the South of England I have seen the old pools in many parts of Sussex and Kent which were used by these forges in days when Sussex was the centre of the English iron industry and the district all along the Weald or forest of Kent and Surrey and Sussex was noted for its furnaces. It was the discovery of coal that caused the iron industry to become centred in Lancashire and other parts of the Midlands.

The bloomaries dated from very ancient times, so ancient that in the Lake District many of these old furnaces were known as " Roman bloomaries," and may have dated from Roman days.

In Western Argyll, the original seat of Gaelic civilisation in the West Highlands, I know of many places bearing ancient names like " Porst na' Ceardaich "—Port of the Smith, or " Alt na' Ceardaich " — Burn of the Smith, and " Bal na' Gown (Gobhain) " — Place or Village of the Smith. By these places many old refuse-heaps have been found connected with the Smith's ancient calling.

In all these old Lakeland forges, of course, charcoal or peat was used, and charcoal-burning is still carried on in the English Lake District.

One of the oldest bloomaries in the north was reopened during the War, at Backbarrow. In the Coniston district the business of charcoal-burning was carried on to supply this forge with charcoal. It is a very ancient trade, and has some interesting customs, one of which is a little surprising—it is the custom of the charcoal-burner to sleep in his clothes. The reason is that the work needs close attention both night and day.

In ancient times coppice wood was grown especially for the charcoal, but the once extensive coppices have mostly disappeared in Lakeland.

The wood is at its best for this purpose in the summer and autumn. It is placed under a covering of turf and is left to smoulder for many hours, twenty-four at least.

The charcoal-burner lives in a hut of ancient pattern and great picturesqueness, and enjoys family life amid the loveliest scenery. Of the tools of his trade—the wood he burns fills the air with a delightful odour which would be envied by town workers, and the bracken with which he kindles his fire is itself one of the great beauties of the fells. His industry is also, one of the healthiest and the charcoal-burner is the cleanest man known, because charcoal is, perhaps, the greatest cleanser known. A charcoal-burner while at work needs no laundry bills. His occupation if not a continual feast is certainly a continual bath.

The charcoal-burner's trade secrets were and still are, handed down from one generation to another and in the secret places of Nature, by lake and wood and planting, he reads her book by night and by day.

The charcoal is made from sapling oak, willow, hazel, etc. The bark is peeled from the wood, and the sticks, which are about the thickness of a man's wrist, are placed over a round pit in the form of a cone which rests on three great

CHARCOAL-BURNING.

stakes. The smaller stakes are placed all round like rafters on a roof. The pit is then filled with charcoal and over these rafters is placed a thatch of thick carpet-grass. The fire is then kindled on the floor of the cone-shaped wigwam. The fire smoulders for about twenty-four hours and has to be watched by the charcoal-burner night and day, because if a flame arises it spoils the charcoal.

After two days the clods of turf are withdrawn and the charcoal is ready. One batch will give about thirty-six bags of charcoal.

In the last stage of their manufacture we have little sticks of charcoal of about the thickness of your thumb. The life of a charcoal-burner is a hard one despite its romance and close contact with the beautiful in Nature. The pay in 1905 was thirty shillings a week.

The charcoal made in the woods at the north end of Coniston Lake was taken down to Nibthwaite Quay at the south end in the boats that plied on the Lake until the railway was opened in 1859. The traffic on the Lake had existed since the time of William de Lancaster, great-great-grandson of Ivo de Tallebois, Lord of Kendal, Windermere, Rydal, Grasmere, Working-

ton, Furness, Amounderness and other districts
of Westmorland, Lancashire, Cumberland and
Lincolnshire.

In the great woods of Furness the bloomaries
were first suspended in 1565, the reason given being
that the " tops and croppings " of the trees were
used for feeding the cattle in winter and could
not be spared. The ash and especially the holly
were used for this purpose. Pennant writing
in 1766 noticed the great parks of holly trees
on the commons. The overcrowding of these
common lands with cattle and ponies, was made
the excuse for the great enclosures of forest lands
by which the rich man was made richer and the
poor man poorer.

CHAPTER XLVIII

SCAWFELL'S MYSTIC CIRCLE

PERHAPS the most wonderful and certainly the
most famous road out of Keswick leads to that
region of grim and fantastic shapes where Scawfell
Pike and Great Gable and the Steeple Rock,
Scawfell, Great End and Bowfell, stand in a
mystic circle, more hidden from the sightseer
than any other mountain range. The view of
Wastwater with Great Gable at its head, a
mountain of rare grace and beauty, is famous,
but the view on turning into it from Wastdale
is finer. And here is the small church which
succeeded an ancient one of no known dedication.

The scene around is extraordinarily grand and
threatening. The Screes rising right up from
the lake impress you with their height and vast-
ness, and completely shut out the sunlight from
east and south for the whole of the three and a

half miles of its length, while Seatallen shuts out
the red and gold of the west.

At Nether Wastdale at the foot (the south end)
of the Lake is another small church which has
succeeded an ancient church whose dedication
was unknown. The seating accommodation was,
I think, for forty-five people. From Nether
Wastdale it is best to take a boat if you wish to
climb Scawfell Pike. From a boat also, a fine
impression of the magnificent surroundings may
be best obtained. The rocks here are of granite
and they lend themselves to all sorts of pillar-
like spikes and spiral forms and grim precipices.

CHAPTER XLIX

ENNERDALE WATER

AND ITS MINING MEMORIES

ENNERDALE LAKE has been called the loveliest of Cumberland's waters. That is saying a good deal, but it is true that it has about it the sense of remoteness, of silence, of austerity. It stands beside ·some of the grandest of the lakeland mountains, in the Wastdale, Scawfell, the Steeple and the Pillar, Great Gable and Melbreak direction.

The Lake is grandly set among bare and rocky hills. Great Gable, one of the most admired and finely placed hills, stands at the head of ·Wastwater and the foot of Ennerdale Lake.

From Red Pike on its bank, no less than five lakes can be seen: Derwentwater, Crummock Water, Lowes Water, Buttermere and Ennerdale itself.

The well - known mines at Ennerdale were discovered by one Martin Boundy, a Cornishman, whose kin had been bred to mining from far-back times. He it was who discovered also the copper on the estate of the Parnell family at Avondale in Ireland. In fact, Mr. Boundy was a genius at finding riches in the earth and should have held a professorship at a university so great were his scientific gifts and his wide knowledge. He had also, other high qualities—splendid personal courage, a very kind heart, and that gift which we all covet—a handsome presence. His eye could flash like a scimitar and he had a complexion like a milkmaid's. His faults were a very independent and fiery spirit, and a not too well-filled pocket, this perhaps because he would not, could not fawn upon the wealthy and the arrogant. He it was who was lowered down with a rope round his waist to examine the lode of copper which he had discovered in the great cliffs at Lough Murragha on the coast of Mayo. He had a lease of the mines and showed his splendid engineering skill in tunnelling and scaffolding on the face of the 1200-feet cliffs. Down these I once went to the little green space beside the ocean far below.

Mr. Boundy was the lessee also, of the copper mines at Srahlaghy some seven miles further inland, across the great bog. There as everywhere he went, he was the wise father of the village —employer, counsellor, medical adviser and sick nurse. Despite the fact that he was ultra-English and ultra-Protestant, among the wholly Irish and Catholic people he was immensely popular in Ireland as he was at Ennerdale.

CHAPTER L

ONLY a little westward from Ambleside and Windermere and south-west of Keswick, we have the highest mountain region of England. You can, I think some one has pointed out, cover all the famous mountain climbs in a twenty-mile circle with Grasmere as a centre.

The chief of these heights are in the Bowfell and Scawfell neighbourhood.

Here the verdure which is so notable by the lakes, disappears. We have rocks and bare hill tops with a little bracken and short heather, on the lower slopes and the mosses and plants characteristic of mountain regions—the Fir Club moss, Staghorn moss (wolf's claw) and Alpine Lady's Mantle and Alpine Club moss. The buzzard hawk I have seen here lately ; forty years ago it was almost extinct in the Lake District.

A capital description of the bird and its habits was given in a popular magazine by my friend Mr. Charles Walmsley of Ambleside some time ago.

In the heart of this region the wealth of bird life disappears ; a single stonechat one climber records having seen in a day's climb, and again a single buzzard, a swift and a stonechat. Of course ravens are to be seen wherever sheep are fed on the hills. Other birds sometimes seen are the dotterel, curlew, peewit, jackdaw and swift.

WRYNOSE PASS AND WASTDALE

If after we have rested in the old house of the Solitary above Blea Tarn we retrace our steps instead of going on to Langdale we can get into this region by taking the ancient highway on which once travelled all the traffic between Kendal and the villages between that town and Whitehaven.

Indeed Whitehaven is a mushroom in growth compared with this ancient track. Probably long before Whitehaven was thought of it was the highway to the Roman Camp or station at Ambleside which Camden identifies, I believe rightly, as the Roman Amboglana.

28

I know there are some who have translated the name as " Hamelsite " or " Hamelside." They were probably not aware that here in this once purely British region the name is quite probably what any Kelt would take it to be—a Keltic word. That is, at any rate, what I believe it to be. *Amhain, bog* and *lan,* taking them on their face value, would be the river of the bog and possibly *llan* a building or place of buildings. Certainly we had here at the Roman town the bog or soft (wet) place.

The Kintyre man says to-day " Tha e bog "— " It is wet—raining " and the Glasgow man says " It's a saft day " an exact translation of the Gaelic of his forebears. " Hamelsite " is what the speaker of English much later made of the name Ambleside, and, indeed, still makes of it for I have heard the men in this year, 1921, in loading luggage into the Lakeland coach use exactly the same phonetic pronunciation.

The road along the valley of the River Brathay to Wrynose Pass is over twelve hundred feet up, at the point where stands the Three Shire Stone. To the north are Black Crag, and Pike o' Blisco, which we saw so finely from Blea Tarn house, and, as we descend we enter the Valley of the Duddon,

BIRKS BRIDGE, DUDDON VALLEY.

famed in song. At Cockley Beck where the Duddon sweeps round southwards, we have Crinkle Crags to the north and Harter Fell (2240)—Birker Moor and the Valley of the Esk, to the south-west; directly before us is Hard Knott (1800). Passing the road to Birker Bridge we ascend to Hard Knott Pass.

From this point we have a grand view of the wildest and most precipitous mountains of Lakeland—Scawfell, Scawfell Pike (3210) immediately north of it, Great End (2984); a little to the east Esk Hause (2370) with Allen Crags (2512), Bowfell (2960). To the west lie the green valleys of the Esk, the Mite, and the Irt in strange contrast to this great central meeting of the barren and desolate moors and mist-haunted, rain-soaked and splintered peaks of central Lakeland.

From Wrynose Pass the old Whitehaven track mounts the long brae to the Roman station of Hardknot.

Hardknot Castle

The castle of Hardknot lies on the bleak heights about 120 feet from the road—one of the loneliest spots in England; but there was no spot too remote for those wonderful people to include in their march, and Hardknot was of great military value as it commanded the only pass into the land of the great British tribe of the Gwynedd, from the north-west.

The camp or castle stands on a prepared plateau, it is square in form, each side being about 130 yards in length. In the centre were two large buildings which may still be traced. There were four gates, at each of which is still a pile of stones. At the four corners were four round towers the foundations of which have been traced. Among the granite stones taken from the mountain side freestone and Roman bricks have been found. The freestone must have been brought from Gosforth a distance of fourteen miles, and the bricks, it has been pointed out, could not have been made at any spot nearer than the village of Drigg. A square plot of land above the camp has been made artificially, and is supposed to have formed the parade ground for the Roman soldiers.

From the castle there is a good view of the Isle of Man and of Eskdale. This is the region of the most difficult climbing. With it one associates many famous names—writers, artists, climbers, men of science.

In the Valley of the Esk there are two waterfalls worth seeing, especially Stanley Ghyll or Gill, and Birker Force which rushes superbly through high granite crags.

To realise the wild beauty and the austerity of these giant hills it is well to continue towards Boot and take the pony track that leads into Wastdale by the foot of Great Gable (2949) then northward through Sty Head Pass and Sty Head Gill to Borrowdale and Keswick. Sty Head (1800) is the highest pass, I think, in England, unless we regard the road through the Nent Valley to Kirkhope as a pass. It reaches 2045 ft.

Wastwater is the deepest of the lakes and is perhaps the most striking and impressive owing to the noble and sharp-pointed mountains lying at its head.

Along one side of it lie the Screes filling the whole valley, and rising sheer out of the dark water. Beyond are Scawfell and Scawfell Pike, Great End, Ling Mell and Great Gable, the latter grandly filling the head of the lake.

On the opposite side are Yewbarrow, Middle Fell and Backbarrow Pike : a veritable meeting-place of the mountains.

It is a grim and barren spot, bleak, desolate,

the constant haunt of rain-clouds which move majestically round the peaks all day, all night—changing ever into new and lovely forms. Forms indeed, so grand and mystical, that the barren scenery is made more lovely than groves of pine or acres of heather and red bracken could have made it.

The view from Scawfell Pike is very extensive—Morecambe Bay, the Scottish hills, Eskdale, Miter Dale, Borrowdale; and of hills Black Combe, Bowfell, Crinkle Crags, the Langdales, Fairfield, Blencathara, Skiddaw, High Street, Ill Bell, Sty Head, Stonethwaite, Great End, Causey Pike, Maiden Mawr, Crummock, Grassmoor, the Pillar Rock, Kirkfell, Lingmell, Red Pike. Also the Irish Sea, the Isle of Man, Hinderscarth, Robinson, Windermere, Coniston Old Man and, indeed, a confusion of mountains such as we can see from no other spot in Lakeland.

From the Pike, Ennerdale or Buttermere can be reached by Black Sail Pass or by Crummock Water and Borrowdale; or a way may be taken from the foot of Crummock Water by the lovely vale of Newlands to Keswick.

In the central region round Scawfell little bird

BLACK SAIL PASS.

life is seen, as has been pointed out, and vegetation ceases save for the marvellously coloured lichens and alpine mosses with their gorgeous yellows and burnt siennas which heighten so much the weird and lovely scene.

INDEX

THE END

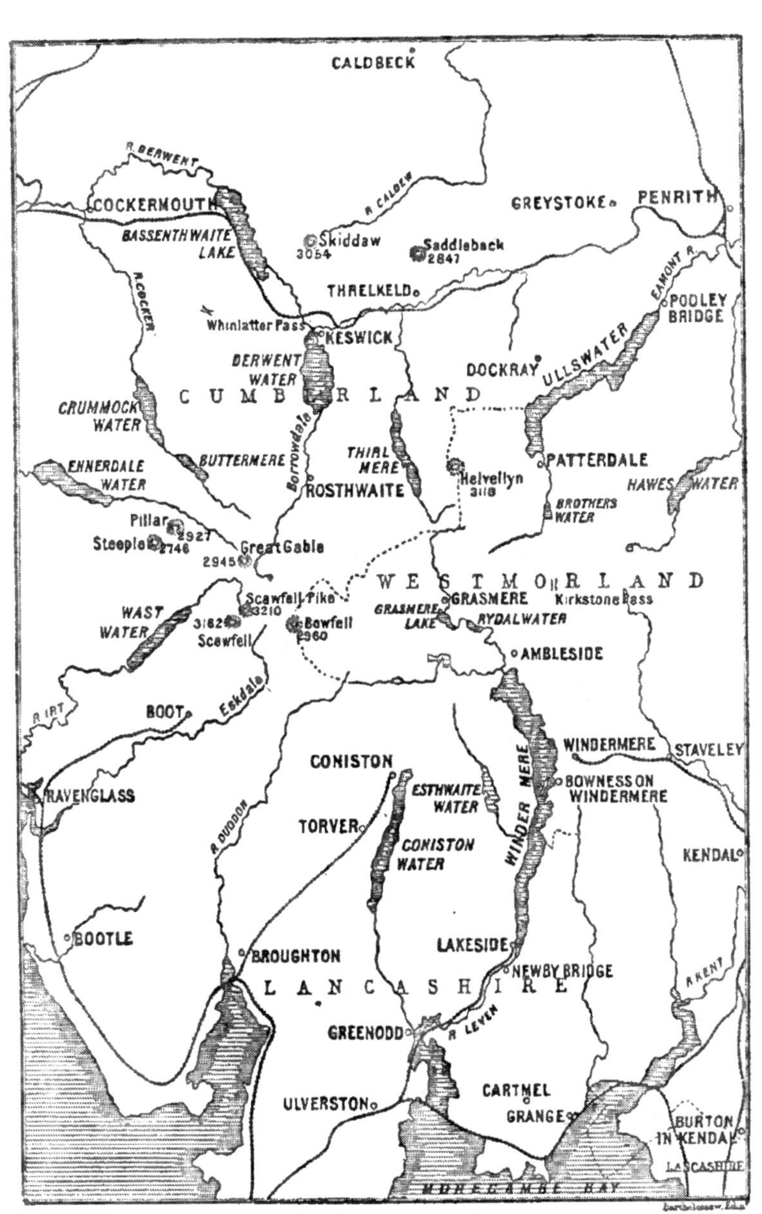

SKETCH MAP OF THE ENGLISH LAKE DISTRICT.

www.ingramcontent.com/pod-product-compliance
Lightning Source LLC
La Vergne TN
LVHW011346180726
843640LV00005B/1171